Y0-BDI-186

Sheila Macqueen's Flowers and Food for Special Occasions

Sheila Macqueen's Flowers and Food for Special Occasions

with recipes by Diana Baldwin

A Hyperion Book Ward Lock Limited · London

Acknowledgments

I would like to thank all those who have helped me so much with this book. Firstly to Diana Baldwin who has made a very large contribution: she accepted the challenge of organizing the menus with enthusiasm and her presentation of the food is quite superb and all done with such calm efficiency. To all the staff at Ward Lock who help in every way they can, and particularly to Suzanne Kendall, who once again added those more than helpful suggestions. To Caroline Mackinlay who always gives her utmost in practical advice, and good humour. To Peter Crawley for yet one more book he has asked me to write for Hyperion Books, and for the great task he did in reading and helping in so many ways.

Lastly, to Roy Smith who once more has produced some of the most lovely photographs, which will delight all those who read and—I hope—use this book. Three of the photographs have been very kindly loaned by 'Flora' magazine, the excellent publication for flower arrangers.

A Hyperion Book
First published in Great Britain in 1980 in association with Peter Crawley
by Ward Lock Limited, 47 Marylebone Lane, London W1M 6AX, a Pentos Company.

Designed by Peter Holroyd
House editor Suzanne Kendall
Text filmset in Monophoto Baskerville
by Advanced Filmsetters (Glasgow) Ltd

Printed and bound in Great Britain by
Butler and Tanner Ltd, Frome and London

British Library Cataloguing in Publication Data

Macqueen, Sheila
Flowers and food for special occasions.—(Hyperion books).
1. Flower arrangement 2. Party decorations
3. Cookery 4. Entertaining
I. Title II. Baldwin, Diana III. Series
745.92'6 SB449.5.P3

ISBN 0-7063-5942-9

Contents

A Glossary for American Readers

apples, cooking—tart
bicarbonate of soda—baking soda
black treacle—molasses or corn syrup
chipolatas—cocktail sausages
cocktail sticks—toothpicks
cornflour—cornstarch
cream, double—heavy
cream, single—light
flour, plain—all-purpose
flour, self-raising—self-rising
golden syrup—maple syrup
icing—frosting
ketchup—catsup
lard—shortening
minced beef—ground beef
muslin—cheese cloth
sugar, demerara —dark brown sugar
sugar, granulated—white
sugar, icing —confectioners'
sugar, soft brown—light brown sugar
sultanas—golden raisins

Notes on ingredients and measurements used in this book: unless specified differently in the recipes the reader should use size 4/ medium eggs, plain flour, level spoon measurements and caster sugar. The recipes cater for six people unless stated otherwise.

Introduction

Having a party at home today is, perhaps, the only way many people can afford to entertain and keep in contact with friends and make life a little more interesting and rewarding. If you live alone it is nice to have friends to visit you and likewise to visit them, but with the present-day cost and difficulty in obtaining help a lot of work is involved, so I hope through this book to give as much practical advice as I can. I have given, wherever possible, short cuts in cooking, ideas for preparation beforehand and for making the maximum use of the deep freeze, and have chosen flowers that can be grown and used with the least trouble and expense. Making a home-made container will add great interest to the table and help with the blending of colours for food and flowers. And, for example, for a dinner party the courses are planned to be well-balanced and not too rich, with dishes intermingled that are both hot and cold and not all extravagant. Suppose that if the main course is to be the luxury of salmon or grouse then the starter can be a delicious but inexpensive cold soup, and the sweet, fruit in season and cream.

Through my early years I learnt a great deal about food from my mother who was a marvellous cook, and even in the years when we had lots of help she would always supervise the making of the sauces, and made the pastry. Then, naturally, my years of working with the late Constance Spry, and subsequently Rosemary Hume, added greatly to my interest and I had the opportunity of developing a feel for food, learning something about wine, much more about presentation and certainly a love for party-giving! So I hope that all this experience will be of some use to you.

Sheila Macqueen

New Year's Eve Party (illustration page 20)

At the New Year one is full of excitement and you really want to forget Christmas and the holly and the ivy. Make a completely fresh start with pinks and blues or, as I have here, with white and pink to get right away from the reds and golds of Christmas time. In America I saw a wonderful party where the tables were decorated with fresh flowers as a base and large bunches of balloons, filled with helium gas! The balloons floated in a bunch about 60 cm/2 ft above the centre of the table flowers and it was quite one of the most effective arrangements I have ever seen. I thought I would like to do this, but I just could not find anyone to supply the gas. So I compromised and wired the balloons and had them just as part of the decor at the back.

I used a silver candelabra, placed a candle in the middle and used two candle cups on either side. These were filled with wet Oasis and tied in with silver wire, then filled with flowers. It is sometimes difficult at New Year to find very much from the garden but it was amazing how much was available when I started looking. I found a few roses, some *Nerine bowdenii*, quite a lot of *Viburnum fragrans* (with a surprising number of blooms) and some hazel catkins. I bought some pink and white carnations, always a good buy nowadays, at any time of the year. Single white chrysanthemums, these are the American spray, which seem to be always with us; rather a pity, really, as I love flowers in season, but they are such useful plants that I don't think that any florist from New York to Sydney could live without them. *Tradescantia albiflora* and small trails of ivy (grown up my sun room wall) completed the arrangements—I find these extremely useful because they trail naturally over the side of the candle cups, so concealing the holders.

It is sad that the use of finger bowls seems to have gone for ever as it is such a nice custom. So little time or trouble is involved, and I love to be able to pick up a delicious leg of pheasant or duck, for the sweetest meat really is nearest the bone! I have placed a few flowers in the finger bowls and best of all are a few leaves of sweetly-scented geraniums as they scent the water as well as the air.

A New Year's Eve party is full of promise, fun and good resolutions. Strangely, it can be one of the longest nights of the year! I found that the first ever New Year's Eve party that I gave was quite exhausting. We started with a buffet serve-yourself party and this went fine—but so quickly that it was all over by nine-thirty and, my goodness, is it a long evening until twelve o'clock! I do not ever remember a longer evening in all my life. So this decided me once and for all that it must be a dinner party. Everyone can sit and enjoy a nice meal and chat and for this reason we have decided on a dinner for six people. This can be doubled very easily for twelve—a good number for a party and one which gives you the chance to make the men change places after the main course.

For the dinner party Diana chose pheasant to make a change from turkey, and though the initial preparation of the dish may seem a bit fiddly, the end result is well worthwhile. The egg mousse is a new recipe for me, made here to cut like a cake, served with a little salad such as watercress and chicory, or it can be made in a mould or ring and served with small strips of celery and can, of course, be used at any time of the year. Meringue is always popular and the honeycomb sweet is one that Diana and I have both been brought up with, coming as we do from the North of Scotland. It is a very good and easy sweet that seems to have become forgotten in recent years and I can thoroughly recommend it. It is served here with caramel oranges, which are most refreshing, and oranges are always good and plentiful at this time of year. The oranges are peeled, sliced and put back on cocktail sticks to look like whole oranges.

Egg Mousse

6 hard-boiled eggs
250 ml/8 fl oz/1 cup mayonnaise (a good bland bought one)
7 g/¼ oz/½ packet powdered gelatine
150 ml/¼ pint/generous ½ cup stock or water
1 teaspoon anchovy essence
pinch of salt and cayenne pepper
80 ml/3 fl oz/6 tablespoons double cream

For the garnish:
pretzel biscuits
1 hard-boiled egg, sliced

Chop the 6 hard-boiled eggs, a potato masher does this job very well, and mix into the mayonnaise. Dissolve the gelatine in the stock or the water and add to the egg mixture with the anchovy essence and the salt and cayenne pepper. Whip the cream until it will just hold its shape and fold it into the egg mixture. Oil a 900 ml/1½ pint/2 US pint mould and pour the mousse mixture into it and leave it to set in a cool place. Turn the mousse out and garnish it with pretzels and a sliced hard-boiled egg.

Georgian Pheasant

225 g/8 oz/2½ cups shelled walnuts
1 kg/2 lb grapes
4 oranges
1 teabag/1 teaspoon green or China tea
1.5 kg/3 lb pheasant
150 ml/5 fl oz/⅔ cup sweet white wine
75 g/3 oz/½ cup butter
salt and pepper
25 g/1 oz/¼ cup plain flour

Pour some boiling water over the walnuts and leave them to stand for a few minutes, then remove the skins using a sharp knife. Put the grapes through a Mouli sieve or liquidize and sieve them. Squeeze the juice from the oranges. Pour 150 ml/¼ pint/¾ cup of boiling water on to the tea, leave to infuse for five minutes and then strain.

Put the pheasant into a large casserole with all the ingredients, omitting the flour and half the butter. Cover the casserole and put into the oven 180°C/350°F/Gas Mark 4 for about an hour or until the pheasant is tender. The exact time will depend on the size and tenderness of the bird. Cut the pheasant into joints and put aside to keep warm. Strain the sauce and put the walnuts on one side, keeping them warm. Mix the remaining butter with the flour to make a paste—this is called Beurre Manié. Bring the sauce to the boil and boil it hard to reduce it by half, to about 500 ml/1 pint/2 cups, then thicken it with the Beurre Manié by whisking it in gradually until the sauce is of the desired thickness. Arrange the pheasant joints in a warm serving dish, pour over the sauce and scatter the walnuts on top.

Serve with Duchesse potatoes.

Duchesse Potatoes

1 kg/2 lb potatoes
1 nut of butter
1 egg yolk
a little hot milk
salt and pepper
1 egg

Boil the potatoes until they are just cooked. Drain well, sieve and return to the pan with the butter, the egg yolk and milk and beat them well to make a firm purée. Season to taste. Have ready a large piping bag fitted with a large vegetable rose pipe and fill it with the purée. Pipe rosettes of potato on to a greased baking tray,* brush them with a beaten egg and bake in a fairly hot oven, 200°C/400°F/Gas Mark 6 for about 20 minutes or until they are golden brown. Use a fish slice to remove them from the tray and put into a warm serving dish.

* They can be frozen at this stage for a maximum of one month.

Pear and Ginger Meringue

3 egg whites
pinch of ground ginger
175 g/6 oz/$\frac{3}{4}$ cup caster sugar

For the filling:
400 ml/$\frac{3}{4}$ pint/1$\frac{3}{4}$ cups double cream
1 tablespoon ginger syrup, from a jar of preserved ginger
1 large can/822 g/1$\frac{3}{4}$ lb pears in quarters

Mark on 3 pieces of non-stick paper or kitchen foil a circle 18 cm/7 in in diameter and place on 3 baking trays.

Whisk the egg whites, using a balloon whisk, until they are very stiff. They should stand up in a stiff peak when held on the whisk. Mix the ground ginger with the caster sugar and whisk in 3 teaspoons of sugar into the egg white and continue to whisk for a few seconds then, using a metal spoon, fold in the rest of the ginger sugar. Be careful not to be over-enthusiastic in folding in the sugar as this can be one of the causes of meringues weeping during cooking. Divide the mixture into three and spread on the marked circles. Bake in a very cool oven, 110°C/225°F/Gas Mark $\frac{1}{4}$ for about two to three hours, or until the meringue discs are dried out and the paper will peel off. You will find they will cook evenly if the trays are changed around in the oven during cooking. Peel off the paper or foil and leave to cool. These meringue discs can be stored in an air-tight tin for a week or two and so may be made well in advance.

Whip the cream until it will hold its shape and flavour it with the ginger syrup.

Sandwich the meringue discs with the cream and the pear quarters, keeping 6 pear quarters and enough cream for the piped decoration. Arrange the 6 pear quarters on the top meringue. Fill a piping bag, fitted with a small vegetable rose pipe, with the remaining cream and pipe rosettes between the pears.

Meringue discs are very useful as they can be sandwiched with any fruit and cream and, of course, they do not have to be flavoured with ginger. Try making chocolate meringues by adding some cocoa powder to the sugar before folding it in.

Honeycomb Ring with Caramel Oranges

2 eggs
75 g/3 oz/⅓ cup caster sugar
15 g/½ oz/1 packet powdered gelatine
750 ml/1¼ pints/3 cups milk
½ teaspoon vanilla essence

Separate the eggs. Cream the egg yolks with the sugar until light then stir in the gelatine. Put the milk into a pan and bring to just under boiling point, pour on to the egg yolk mixture and mix well. Return to the rinsed-out pan and bring back to just under boiling point. Stir in the vanilla essence. Whisk the egg whites until stiff then fold them into the custard. Pour into a 1.2 litre/2 pint/2 US pint ring mould and leave to set overnight. To serve, turn out on to a plate and surround with orange slices and put the reassembled oranges (see next recipe) in the centre.

Oranges in Caramel

For the caramel sauce:
225 g/8 oz/1 cup granulated sugar
150 ml/¼ pint/generous ½ cup cold water
150 ml/¼ pint/generous ½ cup warm water

8 oranges

First make the caramel. Put the sugar and cold water into a pan and warm over a very gentle heat, stirring until all the sugar has dissolved. This is very important—if it is not all dissolved it could crystalize when brought to the boil. Bring to the boil and allow to boil without stirring until it is a rich brown colour. Do not let it get too dark or it might taste burnt. Take it off the heat and, covering your hand with a cloth as the mixture will splash, pour in the warm water, stirring until it melts again. If it does not dissolve quickly, put it back on the heat stirring until it does. Allow it to get cold. This sauce will keep in a screw-top jar so it can be made in advance. To prepare the oranges, cut the rind and pith off the oranges using a serrated-edge knife. Cut into slices and make some into orange shapes by holding them together with cocktail sticks. Pour over the caramel sauce and leave the oranges in the sauce overnight so that they absorb the caramel flavour. When you serve the honeycomb some of the caramel sauce can be served with it.

Gaelic Coffee

whisky
hot, strong black coffee
double cream
sugar

Warm large coffee cups or glasses, and pour a tot of whisky into each. Fill up with hot coffee and add a little sugar and stir—this will make the cream float. Then pour one tablespoonful of cream on to the surface over the back of a teaspoon. Serve at once without stirring.

Lunch Party from the Deep Freeze

(illustration page 21)

I have used here a mixed green arrangement, quite one of my most favourite sorts of flower arrangement. The container is quite inconsequential as it does not show—in point of fact it was a soup tureen from a white dinner service with a green design, but as you can see this is hardly noticeable. A mixture of green seed heads, foliage and flowers makes the right sort of arrangement for a simple lunch, as it is very important to have the flowers so that they blend in with the meal as a whole. Placing some soaked Oasis in the container I then tied a piece of wire netting over the whole so as to keep the stems firmly in place.

The topmost spike is a piece of *Phytolacca americana*—this is an interesting plant and in the green stage lasts well and makes a marvellous 'point'. Next to this is a seed head of *Sisyrinchium striatum*, these turn almost black and are a great asset for a winter dried arrangement. A piece of *Sedum* 'Autumn Joy' is next, still in its green stage which I enjoy almost as much as when it is bright carmine red. Seed heads of *Lunaria annua*—this is an interesting plant in as much as I enjoy it at three different stages; in early spring when it produces a mass of purple flowers, and then as in the photograph when the unopened seed heads turn the most lovely colour—they will dry like this and are even more attractive for me than when they shed the outer coat and become the silvery, transparent round discs that are sold everywhere as Honesty or the Money Plant, universally popular and sold in bunches for winter flower arranging. Poppy seed heads—these are a lovely grey-green and are very popular for winter dried arrangements.

I have included three different *Hosta* leaves. The most unusual and effective is the one on the bottom right, *H. sieboldiana* 'Frances Williams', which must be one of the most wonderful examples of *Hosta* in existence, having a grey-green corrugated leaf with a deep yellow border. On the extreme left is *H. fortunei* 'Yellow Edge' and on the right one that has stayed golden all summer though there is no reason why it should do this. The magnificent green *Arum* (below the poppy seed heads) is 'Green Goddess' whose seeds came from Kenya many years ago and have increased and withstood two really cold winters and are growing outside against a south wall. Seed heads of the herb Lovage are good for culinary use, small amounts may be put in stews and used for salad, but it is for this very attractive seed head that I like it most of all. The large cream and green ivy leaves are *Hedera colchica dentata* 'Variegata', interesting because one is never sure exactly what colour they will be from pure cream to green-blotched cream. Tucked in by the ivy are a few blooms of *Helleborus orientalis* and a few sprays of beech leaves can be seen at the far right and bottom left. The large glossy hand-shaped leaves of *Fatsia japonica* on the left complete the arrangement. These plants have proved to be much more hardy than one first imagined. Mine has withstood three fairly hard winters, and I find I use the leaves all the time.

More and more has been learnt about the characteristics of food so that a meal can be prepared over several days and gradually packed away in the deep freeze to be taken out whenever the mood takes you to have someone in for lunch, or even more important, when someone arrives unexpectedly and there need be no panic. Try as I may I never manage to achieve all the meal as Diana has prepared here, but I do try hard to have one or two things available, and given short notice I can usually produce a starter and maybe a sweet!

Things I find invaluable are pâtés and taramosalata, the Greek dish, but made from smoked cod's roe and butter rather than using oil and breadcrumbs which may be considered the traditional way. Pies are most useful, either meat or fruit; veal and ham pie made with a hot-water crust, cooked and frozen, needs only time to thaw out, whereas steak and kidney and fruit pies are best placed in the freezer uncooked, and these are more valuable for the unexpected guest as they can be placed in the oven direct from the freezer and only need the time necessary for cooking. This, strangely enough, is often quicker than completely thawing out an already cooked dish. One learns by experience how long things take and it is best to give sufficient time as something not quite unfrozen is a real disaster.

The main thing about freezing, especially savoury dishes, is that it is better to under-season rather than over-season them as the freezing process tends to strengthen the seasoning. More can always be added but it cannot easily be taken away. Always make sure that when freezing soups, casseroles, etc., they are completely cold before putting them in. Try and freeze things in square or rectangular containers as they do not waste so much space and are much easier to store. If you have any spare time whilst cooking it is a good idea to make extra pastry or sauces to put in the freezer as this is so much easier than doing everything at the last minute.

For this meal we have chosen a spicy tomato soup and veal and ham pie. The raised pie (which can be served hot or cold) is a lot easier than it looks, the special raised pie mould helps its appearance a lot, but if one is not available an ordinary loose-bottomed cake tin will be just as good. There is no hard-boiled egg in this pie as they do not freeze at all well, the white resembling a piece of indiarubber when it comes out! If egg is preferred in the pie, do not freeze it. The sweet is a speciality that I had in the United States and as it was in a restaurant I had not the courage to ask how it was done! However, I noted the ingredients and we have made our own version, which tastes very like the original, is easy to prepare and so good to eat, especially as an accompaniment to fresh stewed apricots.

Spicy Tomato Soup

25 g/1 oz/2 tablespoons butter
100 g/4 oz/⅔ cup onion
15 g/½ oz/1 tablespoon plain flour
1 teaspoon paprika pepper
1 kg/2 lb tomatoes (if canned, 795 g/23 oz)
1.2 litres/2 pints/5 cups chicken stock
1 large bay leaf
1 bouquet garni
1 clove of garlic
½ teaspoon Worcestershire Sauce
salt and pepper
pinch of sugar
20 g/¾ oz/5 US teaspoons sago
100 ml/4 fl oz/½ cup red wine or port

Melt the butter and add the chopped onion and soften it without letting it brown, add the flour and paprika and cook for a few seconds. Add the tomatoes (quartered if fresh), the stock, bay leaf, bouquet garni, crushed clove of garlic, Worcestershire Sauce, seasoning—remembering to slightly under-season—and sugar. Bring to the boil and simmer for about 30 minutes. Put through a Mouli sieve, return it to a clean pan and add the sago and simmer it for a further 30 minutes or until the sago is cooked. Add the wine and serve.

Veal and Ham Pie

750 g/1½ lb pie veal
1 kg/2 lb cooked bacon, hock or collar
grated rind of half a lemon
salt and freshly ground black pepper
pinch of oregano and mixed herbs
600 ml/1 pint/2½ cups stock, made with a knuckle of veal, or with 15 g/½ oz/1 packet of gelatine dissolved in it

For the pastry:
600 g/1¼ lb/5 cups plain flour
2 teaspoons salt
220 g/7½ oz/1 cup lard
200 ml/7 fl oz/¾ cup water
1 egg

Pre-heat the oven to 200°C/400°F/Gas Mark 6. This pastry must be made and used quickly whilst it is still warm. Prepare the filling first. Cut the veal and bacon into fairly small cubes and put into a bowl, add the grated lemon rind, the seasoning and herbs and mix well together.

Now make the pastry. Sift the flour and the salt into a mixing bowl and make a well in the centre. Put the lard and water into a pan and bring to the boil and pour immediately into the well in the flour, mix it well with a knife, then knead with the hands until it is smooth. Cut off a quarter for the lid and keep it in a warm place until needed. Place a raised pie mould (or cake tin 15–17 cm/6–7 in in circumference) on a baking tray, put in the pastry covering the bottom and working it up round the sides, keeping it as even as possible, to finish level with the top of the mould. Put in the filling, roll out the lid and put on top, sealing the edges. Make a couple of holes in the lid with the point of a knife, roll out the trimmings of pastry, cut into leaf shapes and decorate the top. Brush the top of the pie with the beaten egg to glaze and put into the oven and bake for 40 minutes at 200°C/400°F/Gas Mark 6, then reduce the heat to 180°C/350°F/Gas Mark 4 for a further 40–50 minutes. Leave the pie to cool a little, then pour in the jellied stock through one of the holes, using a pie funnel. Do not allow it to overflow. Leave to cool thoroughly before freezing. Turn out and serve with tomato salad and new buttered potatoes.

San Antonio Ice Cream

60 g/2½ oz/¼ cup granulated sugar
80 ml/3 fl oz/6 tablespoons water
3 egg yolks (size 3/large)
600 ml/1 pint/2½ cups single cream
1 teaspoon vanilla essence
100 g/4 oz/1 cup chopped salted peanuts

Dissolve the sugar in the water and bring it to the boil. Boil it until the thread stage is reached—when a little cool syrup between the fingers forms a thread as the fingertips are parted. Whisk the egg yolks, then pour on the syrup and whisk (using rotary or electric hand whisk) until thick and mousse-like. Pour in the cream and the vanilla essence and mix well.

Pour the mixture into a plastic container and put into the freezer or ice-making compartment of the refrigerator turned to the coldest setting, and leave to thicken, stirring it every half hour or so. When it is thick, add the roughly chopped salted peanuts and return to the freezer to ripen and mellow. If an electric ice cream maker is available, pour the mixture into it and freeze until the mixture is thick and the paddles stop. Take the mixture out and stir in the roughly chopped salted peanuts, put back into the freezer and leave to mellow as before.

Serve with chocolate fudge sauce (see next recipe).

Chocolate Fudge Sauce

90 g/3½ oz/bar of plain chocolate
80 ml/3 fl oz/6 tablespoons water
60 g/2½ oz/generous ⅓ cup sugar
2 tablespoons sweetened condensed milk

Break up the chocolate and dissolve in the water over a gentle heat, add the sugar and when it has dissolved bring it to the boil and allow to simmer for 10–15 minutes, then stir in the condensed milk. Serve either hot or cold.

Gooseberry and Elderflower Water Ice

600 ml/1 pint/2½ cups water
375 g/12 oz/1¾ cups sugar
450 g/1 lb gooseberries
2 heads of elderflower
1 egg white

Put the water and sugar into a pan and dissolve, add the topped and tailed gooseberries and boil until they are tender, about 10 minutes, then add the elderflowers and leave to infuse for 3 minutes. Remove the flower heads, sieve the fruit (or liquidize and sieve) and allow the purée to cool. When it is cold pour into an ice cream maker and freeze until firm. Stir in the stiffly whisked egg white and return the mixture to the freezer to mellow. If you are using a refrigerator, pour the purée into a container and put into the freezer or frozen food compartment turned to its lowest setting. When it begins to freeze around the edges give it a good stir with a fork and put back for another hour. Stir in the whisked egg white and return to freezer to mellow.

Water ices keep well but it is best to take them out of the freezer and put into the refrigerator for an hour before serving so that they can soften slightly.

Spring Dinner Party

For a long time I have wanted to use these swan vases for a dinner party, they are nearly all from a collection that belongs to a friend of mine—their home is on top of a pelmet over a long window! If it had been possible I would like to have had them photographed running down the centre of the table, and for greater effect, perhaps, to have had them placed on a mirror or a piece of mirrored glass. The mirror tiles one can buy to fix to a bathroom wall would have been ideal.

The swans were filled with a mixture of pinks and reds; geraniums, *Crassula*, with clusters of deep pink flowers, small pieces of *Alstroemeria ligtu* hybrid, posies of the little quilled daisy *Bellis perennis*. I also included honeysuckle, pansies, periwinkles, *Petasites* and *Tradescantia*.

I think it would look equally well at any time of year as long as the flowers were small enough and kept in proportion. With small vases it is important to make sure that the flowers do not overpower the containers—it is too easy to do but if you bear in mind that you should keep the vase well in view you will prevent this from happening. These little swans would be very effective arranged with a mass of flowers all of one type; try using lily of the valley, or primroses or snowdrops. Any of these would look enchanting. I love to have arrangements of all one type of flower, but as one is trying often not to take too much colour from the garden, it is easier to pick a little bit of this and a little of that, making a mixed bouquet.

I love a few sweetly scented flowers on the table and though some people feel that too strong a scent takes from the flavour of the food, I cannot say I have ever been really aware of this. Spring is a yellow time and if you cannot use decorative containers like the swans on the table nothing is prettier than baskets of daffodils. These can be arranged not only for the table but also for the rest of the room or even the house.

I well remember a little church near my home arranged for Easter with baskets of daffodils everywhere—on the windowsills, in the porch, on the church steps—I have never seen anything prettier.

If you are really going to town on the flowers then it is nice to have all the dining room flowers, perhaps, in the same colouring which can be carried through the house, but it takes a lot of doing and unless you have a lot of flowers from the garden it could be very expensive at this time of year!

After the long winter months, the arrival of spring with its fresh vegetables gives more choice in the selection of the menu. What could be nicer than asparagus soup made with fresh asparagus!

Asparagus Soup

450 g/1 lb asparagus
1 small onion, chopped
900 ml/1½ pints/1 US quart chicken stock
25 g/1 oz/3 tablespoons butter
20 g/¾ oz/2 tablespoons plain flour
salt and pepper

Liaison:
2 egg yolks
65 ml/2½ fl oz/5 tablespoons single cream

garnish—fried croûtons

Wash the asparagus and cut off the tough white ends, cut into 2.5 cm/1 in pieces. Put into a pan with the onion and the stock, cover and simmer until the asparagus is tender. Keep a few of the tips to garnish the soup, put the rest through a liquidizer and sieve it to remove the coarse bits. Rinse out the saucepan and melt the butter, add the flour and pour on the sieved liquid and season. Bring to the boil and let it simmer for 2–3 minutes.* Blend the yolks and the cream together, add a little of the hot soup to it, stir well then add the mixture to the soup and reheat very carefully. Do not let the soup boil once the liaison has been added otherwise it will curdle. Add the reserved asparagus tips.

To make the bread croûtons. Cut into cubes 2 or 3 slices of bread, preferably stale, and fry in deep fat.

* The soup may be frozen at this stage before the liaison is added.

Chicken Kiev

These are basically the suprême of a chicken, i.e., the breast and wings of a chicken stuffed with parsley-flavoured butter, rolled in egg and breadcrumbs and deep-fat fried. Allow plenty of time to prepare them as they are rather fiddly! You can prepare as far as the egg and crumbing stage the day before or the pieces may be frozen. If they have been frozen allow them to thaw out completely before frying.

Although it does seem extravagant to use only the breasts of the chickens, a casserole or curry can be made with the remainder.

175 g/6 oz/¾ cup unsalted butter
grated rind and juice of a small lemon
4 tablespoons chopped parsley
3 × 1.2 kg/2½ lb roasting chickens
plain flour, seasoned with salt and freshly ground black pepper

1 egg
dried white breadcrumbs
fat for frying
watercress for garnish

Cream the butter and gradually work in the lemon rind, the juice and chopped parsley, shape into a pat and leave in the refrigerator to harden.

Cut the suprêmes off the chickens. Using a sharp knife close to the bone, ease the meat off. When the wing joint is reached, cut through the joint and remove the suprême. Leave the wing bone in to give it shape, but cut off the wing pinions. Repeat on the other side of the bird.

Lay the suprême on a board, cover with a piece of waxed paper and flatten it slightly with the back of a heavy knife or a light rolling pin. Cut the butter into six fingers and lay one in the middle of a suprême. Wrap the suprême round the butter. It should stay in shape on its own but if not secure with a cocktail stick. Roll in seasoned flour. Brush with the beaten egg and roll in the breadcrumbs, pressing them on firmly. Repeat with the other suprêmes.*

Heat the fat or oil to 190°C/375°F (or until a piece of bread, when dropped in the fat, browns in 20 seconds) and fry the chicken for about 6 minutes until golden brown. It is better to fry them in two sessions for if too many are put in at once the fat will lose its heat. Drain well on kitchen paper, put a cutlet frill on each wing bone, arrange in a serving dish and garnish with a bunch of watercress.

Serve with new potatoes and any other spring vegetable.

* At this stage they can be refrigerated or frozen. Thaw completely before deep frying.

Charlotte Russe

600 ml/1 pint/2½ cups lemon jelly
glacé cherries
diamonds of angelica
12 sponge fingers
300 ml/½ pint/1¼ cups milk
1 vanilla pod or few drops vanilla essence
3 egg yolks
1 tablespoon/1 generous US tablespoon caster sugar
20 g/¾ oz/1½ packets powdered gelatine
3 tablespoons water
300 ml/½ pint/1¼ cups double cream

Make up the jelly as instructed on the packet, and when it is cool pour a little into the bottom of a charlotte tin 900 ml/1½ pint/1 US quart or an 18 cm/7 in round deep cake tin, to the depth of 2.5 cm/1 in and leave to set. When it has set arrange the glacé cherries and the angelica on top of the jelly, then carefully spoon over a little more jelly, and leave to set. Allow the rest of the jelly to set to use for decoration.

Trim the sides of the sponge fingers and fit closely round the sides of the tin.

Scald the milk with the vanilla pod if it is being used. Cream the egg yolks with the sugar until light and creamy. Pour on the milk, removing the vanilla pod, stir well then return to the rinsed out pan. Stir over gentle heat until the mixture coats the back of the spoon. On no account allow it to boil otherwise it will curdle. If this should happen, pour the custard into a cold basin and whisk rapidly for a few minutes. Strain the custard into a basin. Soak the gelatine in the water and stir into the hot custard, adding the vanilla essence if it is being used. Allow to cool.

Whip the cream until it will just hold its shape and when the custard begins to set, lightly fold in the cream. To hasten the setting stage, stand the bowl of custard in a basin of cold water to which a few ice-cubes have been added. Pour into the prepared tin and leave to set.

To turn out the charlotte, quickly dip the base of the tin in hot water, and turn out on to a plate. If liked, the extra jelly can be chopped and put around the base of the charlotte. If the sponge fingers stand above the mixture in the tin, they can easily be trimmed before turning the charlotte out.

Brunch or a Lazy Sunday Lunch

(illustration page 24)

Brunch as the name implies is, of course, a combination of breakfast and lunch and, I feel, will soon be as popular in Britain as it is in America. I was interested to see on my last visit that brunch was advertised in nearly all the clubs and many of the hotels in the United States. If one likes to have a long lie in on Sundays, or when on holiday, no sooner has one had breakfast than one is having to prepare lunch. Cutting out breakfast allows the sporty members of the family to go and play golf, or tennis, squash or what you will, and for those who feel that Sunday can be a late start that extra time having a cup of tea in bed with the Sunday papers is very relaxing and enjoyable,. You will feel really ready for this meal at twelve o'clock and you can then take on all the tasks in the garden during a long afternoon!

Flower arrangements for this casual meal can be quite simple. Here I was so lucky to be given these stems of fasciated *Oenothera* or Evening Primrose, found by a friend of mine in the swamp lands near to Savannah, most extraordinary and only growing on this one plant. She has been able to make the trek on two successive years and found them growing on both occasions. They really are spectacular and I have never seen anything quite like them before and don't expect I will again.

The small 'Singapore' orchids which now seem to be available for many months in the year come in many shades and I like these subtle browny-green ones so much. I think they are generally more popular than the deep purple, which is the colour I always imagine they will be; they are exported all over the world. They last extremely well and are a very good investment—I had these two stems for nearly three weeks. I also included some *Gerbera jamesonii*, *Clivia miniata* and *Cymbidium* for added colour.

All the flowers are arranged on a flat, buff-coloured Australian wooden platter. The flowers and dried pieces are held in place by a large Japanese well pin-holder, which holds enough water for the fresh flowers. My second choice for an occasion like this would have been fruit or vegetables, so decorative and attractive for a simple meal, yet with the warmth and colour that picks up all the browns and yellows of the food. Shiny brown-skinned onions, mushrooms and even potatoes of good shape and colour, a coconut, russet apples, all add interest and different textures for this type of arrangement. Usually fruit can be supported by being piled up one on the other, but if for any reason you feel they might slip or for effect you want to place them higher than you feel they would stand normally, then you can impale them on to each other with cocktail sticks. If you are adding fresh flowers to a fruit arrangement then you will need a separate container to hold enough water for just a few blooms. This can be a small bowl like a soup bowl and you place into it some wet Oasis, tie it down with either Sellotape (Scotch Tape) or string so that it does not show when you have finally finished the arrangement, and keep it well topped up with water for as long as you want it to stay fresh.

Many of the recipes are useful for other meals as well, such as Sunday night supper, luncheons or for an after-the-theatre party, being mostly food that is prepared previously and can be warmed through at a later date. Of course you don't have to make the bread rolls though they really are delicious, and strangely enough, easy to make. Sautéd kidneys are a super dish for breakfast or lunch. Eggs *en cocotte* with a little tomato ketchup or lightly fried mushrooms in the bottom of the cocotte make an excellent starter for a dinner party, or as a main course for lunch with a fresh green salad.

Bread Rolls

Below are two methods of making bread rolls and either method can be used for white or brown rolls. The first method is the quick way, using a vitamin C tablet which cuts out the long rising. For this method, fresh yeast *must* be used. The second method is the usual way and either fresh or dried yeast may be used.

Brown Rolls (using a vitamin C tablet)

450 g/1 lb/4 cups wholemeal flour
250 g/½ lb/2 cups strong white flour
(or all wholemeal can be used)
2 teaspoons/3 US teaspoons salt
7.5 g/¼ oz/1½ teaspoons sugar
15 g/½ oz/1 tablespoon lard
1 × 25 mg vitamin C tablet
400 ml/¾ pint/1¾ cups warm water
25 g/1 oz/1½ packets *fresh* yeast

Put the flour, salt and sugar into a warmed bowl, add and rub in the lard. Crush the vitamin C tablet and dissolve in the warm water with the yeast. Make a well in the flour, pour in the liquid and mix to a dough. Knead it on a floured board for at least 5 minutes, or longer if you can manage it! Leave the dough to stand covered with a polythene bag or sheet of greaseproof paper for 10–15 minutes before shaping. Meanwhile grease a baking sheet and turn on the oven to 220°C/425°F/Gas Mark 7. Divide the dough into roughly 50 g/2 oz pieces and shape into rolls. Put on to the greased baking trays, cover with a polythene bag or greaseproof paper and move them into a warm place to prove for about 10–15 minutes. Remove the bag and place in the preheated oven and bake the rolls for 20 minutes or until they are nicely brown. This quantity will make about 20 rolls.

White Rolls

15–20 g/½–¾ oz/1 packet fresh yeast *or*
7.5 g/¼ oz/½ packet dried yeast
400 ml/¾ pint/1¾ cups warm water
750 g/1½ lb/6 cups strong white flour
¾ dessertspoon/1 US dessertspoon salt
1 generous teaspoon caster sugar
25 g/1 oz/2 tablespoons lard

Dissolve the fresh yeast in the warm water. (Follow the instructions on the tin or packet if using dried yeast.) Sift the flour with the salt and sugar into a warmed bowl, and rub in the lard. Make a well in the centre of the flour, pour in the yeast liquid and mix in a little of the surrounding flour to make a batter. Cover this 'batter' with some more of the surrounding flour and leave in a warm place until the yeast breaks through the flour which was sprinkled on top. Mix in the rest of the flour and knead on a floured surface for at least 10 minutes, or until the dough is smooth, and when a finger is pressed into it the depression

it makes springs up straight away. Place the dough in a greased large bowl, covered as for the brown rolls and put it somewhere warm, the airing cupboard is ideal, until it has doubled in bulk. This takes about 1½ hours. Meanwhile, grease the baking trays. When the dough has risen, knead it again for a minute or two then divide it into about 50 g/2 oz pieces and shape into rolls. Place on the greased trays, cover again, put in a warm place to prove and turn on the oven to 220°C/425°F/Gas Mark 7. After proving for 10–15 minutes put the trays in the preheated oven for 15–20 minutes or until the rolls are golden brown. Cool on a wire tray. This quantity will make about 20 rolls.

* Both the brown and white rolls freeze very well. When they are cold put them into polythene bags and freeze. They are best thawed by heating in the oven half an hour to an hour before they are needed. They will come out with crisp crusts, yet soft and deliciously warm inside.

Sautéd Kidneys

12 lamb kidneys
40 g/1½ oz/3 tablespoons butter
1 small onion
50 g/2 oz/½ cup mushrooms
1½ tablespoons plain flour
300 ml/½ pint/1¼ cups stock
4 slices of bread

Cut the kidneys in half and remove the cores. Heat the butter in a pan and brown the kidneys, take them out and keep them warm. Put the chopped onion into the pan and cook until it begins to brown, then add the mushrooms and cook for a minute or two. Add the flour, cooking it for a few minutes, pour on the stock and stir until it comes to the boil, season, then return the kidneys to the pan and simmer for 10–15 minutes. While the kidneys are cooking, fry the bread in a little hot fat. Cut the slices into half diagonally. Pour the kidneys into a hot dish, and arrange the fried bread triangles around the side.

Kedgeree

350 g/12 oz smoked haddock or a mixture of fresh and smoked haddock
225 g/8 oz/1 cup long grain rice
100 g/4 oz/½ cup butter
3 hard-boiled eggs
salt and pepper
pinch of cayenne pepper
1–2 tablespoons cream
chopped parsley

Poach the fish in water for about 10–15 minutes, then break it into flakes, removing any bones. Cook the rice in plenty of boiling salted water for 12–15 minutes or until it is just cooked, then drain it well.

Melt the butter in a pan, add the flaked fish, the chopped hard-boiled eggs and the cooked rice, and heat thoroughly stirring it gently with a fork. Season to taste. At the last minute, stir in the cream. Turn it into a hot dish and sprinkle with the chopped parsley.

Alternatively, the kedgeree ingredients can be left to cool separately and be heated up later in the oven. Melt the butter in an ovenproof dish, add the flaked fish, chopped egg and the rice, cover and put into a moderate oven for about 20–30 minutes. Before serving, stir in the cream and sprinkle with chopped parsley.

Eggs *en cocotte* with Bacon and Mushrooms

butter
6 eggs
450 g/1 lb bacon rashers
450 g/1 lb mushrooms

Turn the oven to 220°C/425°F/Gas Mark 7. Put a small knob of butter into each of six cocotte dishes, put the dishes on a baking tray and place in the oven to melt. When the butter has melted, take the dishes out of the oven, break an egg into each dish and return to the oven until they are just cooked, which will take about 5–10 minutes. While they are cooking, fry the bacon, and sauté the mushrooms in butter.

When the eggs are cooked, arrange the cocottes round the edge of an oval dish and the bacon and mushrooms in front as in the photograph.

As well as the above dishes, serve a selection of breakfast cereals, grapefruit and fruit juices. Also, offer toast and oatcakes with butter, honey and marmalade.

Oatcakes

300 g/10 oz/1¾ cups oatmeal, fine or medium
1 teaspoon salt
50 g/2 oz/¼ cup lard
150 ml/¼ pint/generous ½ cup hot water

Switch the oven to 190°C/375°F/Gas Mark 5.

Mix the oatmeal and salt together, and make a well in the centre. Put the lard in the hot water to melt then pour this into the oatmeal and mix well to make a stiff paste. Turn on to a floured surface and, working quickly, roll the dough out to about 5 mm/¼ in thick. Either cut into rounds, using a 7.5 cm/3 in plain cutter, or into two 20 cm/8 in rounds and divide these into quarters (or, to give the correct name, farls), then put on to ungreased baking trays and place in the preheated oven for 15–20 minutes. Cool on a wire rack.

The Golden Wedding (illustration page 28)

What a great celebration this undoubtedly is, fifty years of marriage with all the delights, and inevitable heartbreaks that must happen as well. It is a very rewarding occasion filled with memories, celebrated with friends and family who have been part of your lives for fifty years. A time for the very young and the old to mix together. Diana and I decided to make it lunch because of this and because, naturally, elderly people are not so anxious to go out at night. However, the meal we have planned could be eaten at any time of day. We have tried to think of some unusual food and flower settings and for this golden occasion we have chosen 'All Gold' for drinks, food and flowers. I cannot tell you how pretty it looked, and hope you will be able to get the feeling from the photograph. The age of the people concerned is of major importance, and food has to be carefully chosen to suit both the young and the old. So for this occasion all the food should be light yet appetizing and attractive to look at. Melon, orange and grapefruit cocktail; sole with a golden sauce, and yellow saffron rice. A delicious apricot muscovite for sweet, and Buck's fizz to complete the picture. Buck's fizz is made from the juice of one orange, or equivalent, with the glass filled up with champagne and crushed ice, all in keeping with our golden theme.

The idea behind the posies was that all the ladies could take one home, old and young are alike in enjoying doing this! I used ready-made posy frills, which are quite easy to buy. I placed a small piece of Oasis in a small section of a polythene bag behind each frill and attached them to the frills with wire. It is then quite easy to make holes in the polythene with a sharp pair of scissors. In this way all the firm-stemmed flowers were easy to stick in, and those with soft stems were given the assistance of a florist's wire.

I used as many firm-stemmed flowers as possible to keep wiring to a minimum! The roses were 'Allgold', 'Golden Showers', 'Jocelyn' and some buds of 'Apricot Nectar'. The small green flower sprays were of *Alchemilla mollis* which is one of my favourites. The posies could equally well be made with small-sized carnations—the new small spray carnations are really marvellous value for they last until the final bud has opened in water, and can be bought all the year round. Or some single chrysanthemum blooms as these, too, are continuously available. I thought how pretty it would be to have posies of primroses, but the difficulty is that they have such delicate small stems that they do not press easily into the Oasis and so would quickly fade.

The posies were attached to the tall brass church candlestick, with gold ribbons. Make as many as you need for your guests: in any case you need three on each side of the table and the candlestick. Another idea would be to place them round the base of the candelabra, or a storm lantern, placing the rest casually down the table. For the most pleasing effect always see that the ribbons all start from a central point at the base of the candelabra, or you lose the continuity and the general effect appears disjointed. The posies look more effective placed back to back. As with any flower arrangement, be sure and give your flowers several hours in deep water, overnight if possible. Roses, I find, last much better if the ends of the stems are placed in a little boiling water for a few seconds and then allowed to drink.

I made up the little posies and put them in a plastic bag overnight. I find that by

keeping the air away from them, they last for ages without actually being in water, and of course the Oasis is wet. Take them out next day and put them into their frills and attach them to the candlestick by their ribbons. In this way you can make them at leisure and not have a frantic last-minute rush.

I have found that this method of placing arrangements in a plastic bag and the constant overhead spraying, or misting, of the vases really helps to keep flowers fresh much longer. It is particularly useful in the hot weather, as flowers naturally lose moisture more quickly in the summer days than they do when the temperature is colder. Place all vases when possible in the cool overnight or failing that, spray and then cover them completely with a light plastic bag. Always remove any dead flowers, everyday if necessary, and replace—never remove all the flowers from the vases until they are really dead. It is amazing how long they will last in this way if you top up with water and replace the dead or dying flowers.

Melon, Orange and Grapefruit Cocktail

1 melon
2 oranges
2 grapefruit
a little sugar

Using a serrated knife cut the peel and the pith off the oranges and the grapefruit and divide them into segments. To do this, cut through the skin on each side of the segment of fruit and ease it out. Cut the top off the melon and take out the seeds. With a potato baller, or a teaspoon, scoop out the flesh being careful not to make a hole in the skin. Mix the melon flesh with the orange and grapefruit segments and sprinkle on a little caster sugar. A little sherry may be added, if you wish. Put all of the fruit back in the melon, replace the top and stand the melon on ice cubes in a serving dish.

Sole Souchet with Saffron Rice

For the farce:
350 g/12 oz fresh haddock fillet
1 egg white
100 ml/4 fl oz/½ cup double cream
salt and pepper

6 fillets of sole
80 ml/3 fl oz/6 tablespoons white wine, fairly dry
lemon juice—a squeeze
2 tablespoons single cream
salt and pepper
4–6 mushrooms

Béchamel sauce:
25 g/1 oz/2 tablespoons butter
20 g/¾ oz/2 tablespoons plain flour
400 ml/¾ pint/1¾ cups milk
salt and pepper

First prepare the farce. Skin the haddock and put through mincer. Lightly whip egg white, add the fish, beat in the double cream and season to taste.

Skin the sole fillets and lay on a board, skinned side up, and spread the farce over them. Fold in half and neaten the edges. Arrange in a buttered, ovenproof dish, pour over the wine and lemon juice and cover with greaseproof paper. Place in a preheated oven 180°C/350°F/Gas Mark 4 for 12–15 minutes.

While the sole is cooking prepare the sauce. Melt the butter in a saucepan, add the flour and stir over the heat for a few seconds only, stir in milk, bring to the boil stirring all the time and season.

Wipe and slice mushrooms and cook in a little butter. Keep warm. When the stuffed fillets are cooked remove them from the liquid, drain on kitchen paper, arrange on a serving dish and keep hot.

Strain the liquid the fish was cooked in into the béchamel sauce and simmer until it is a creamy consistency, then add the cream. Coat the fillets with the sauce and decorate with the mushrooms. Serve with saffron rice.

Saffron Rice

pinch of saffron
150 ml/¼ pint/generous ½ cup boiling water
350 g/12 oz/1¾ cups long grain rice

Put the saffron into a small basin, pour on boiling water and infuse for 10 minutes. Then strain, keeping the liquid which will be yellow in colour. Cook the rice for about 15–20 minutes in boiling water to which saffron water has been added. Drain and pour boiling water over the rice to remove any excess starch.

Apricot Muscovite

175 g/6 oz/1 cup firmly packed dried apricots
scant 15 g/½ oz/1 packet gelatine
juice of half a lemon
3 egg yolks
75 g/3 oz/⅓ cup caster sugar
300 ml/½ pint/1¼ cups milk
150 ml/¼ pint/generous ½ cup double cream
75 g/3 oz/⅓ cup granulated sugar
150 ml/¼ pint/generous ½ cup water
extra cream for decoration

Soak the apricots overnight in twice their volume of water. Next day cook for 30 minutes or until tender in the same liquid with a strip of lemon rind added. Rub through a sieve, or liquidize and strain. Allow to cool.

Put the gelatine to soak in the lemon juice with 2–3 tablespoons of water.

Cream the egg yolks and the caster sugar together until light and thick. Scald the milk and pour on to the creamed yolk mixture, blend well, return to the pan (which has been rinsed out) and stir continuously over a gentle heat until the mixture thickens—do not let it boil. The custard should coat the back of a spoon. Strain and cool. Melt the gelatine over a gentle heat and add it to the custard. When it has cooled, lightly whip the cream so that it just leaves a trail and fold into it 250 ml/8 fl oz/1 cup of the apricot purée and then fold this into the custard. Pour into an oiled mould 1.2 litres/2 pints/5 cups and leave to set.

Dissolve the granulated sugar in the water, bring to the boil then add the remaining apricot purée and allow to get cold.*

Turn the Muscovite on to a serving dish and pour round some of the sauce, serving the rest in a sauce jug. Decorate with the extra whipped cream.

* This dish may be frozen for a maximum of one week.

Summer Buffet Luncheon (illustration page 32)

Some years ago in the Hilton Hotel in London, to celebrate the appointment of a new manager, they gave the most magnificent party with guests from all their hotels around the world. Apart from the wonderful food and masses of superb flowers everywhere, what appealed to me most were the ice sculptures. They really were works of art—sculptures of swans and ducks and large animals, some so tall they towered above me, moulded and carved most beautifully. All of them were made by chefs in the cold of a freezer so that they did not melt and they were brought out only seconds before the guests arrived. They were a sight I will never forget.

I was delighted to find the moulds from which the sculptures were made the next time I visited America. I have not seen them in Britain yet but have no hesitation in mentioning them as they are bound to be around before too long, as most things filter through in time. I thought the sculptures were amazingly effective and to my delight many lasted through a longish dinner party before they started to drip. They are made in plastic containers which are filled with water which may or may not be coloured. They are hung upside down by strong wires in the deep freeze for twelve hours. The plastic cover has then to be removed with great care—rather like peeling off a rubber glove—so as to be sure you do not decapitate the bird!

The soft pinks and whites of this arrangement are lovely colourings for this time of year, restful and refreshing. It is strange how colours go with the time of year, yellow in spring, mauves and blue in July, orange and golds in August and September. It is hard to beat green and white as a colour scheme at any time and for the cool effect on a hot summer day it is ideal. This arrangement produced a truly lovely effect with delicate summer dishes of food to complement the flowers.

Valuable in any garden, whether one is a flower-arranger or not, are the cream and green spikes of the variegated phlox 'Norah Leigh'. Perhaps I have had uncommon success with this plant, but I must say that it grows with vigour and produces masses of this lovely variegated foliage and dear little pale pink flowers with a deep pink eye. It is a constant delight and is eye-catching all summer. I find it does better when split up regularly every year, removing the hard woody core of the plant which is common to all the phlox family. The *Astrantia major involucrata* is seen at the back of the arrangement, its particularly long shaggy segments and pale greenish colour at the tips of the fluffy heads are so pretty but sadly, unlike other members of the *Astrantia* family, it does not seed freely, so the only way to propagate it is by division. The beautiful mock orange, 'Belle Etoile' in a cluster at the base of the vase, is an outstanding *Philadelphus*, with open white, many-stamened, sweetly-scented flowers. These have a purple blotch at the base of the petals and are a 'must' for the shrub border. They last better in water if you remove all the leaves to reveal the delicate flowers.

Of the roses, 'Elizabeth Harkness' is the larger open rose at the top of the vase, creamy-white, quite beautiful and, as Jack Harkness will tell you, it has to be superb as it is named after his only daughter. The other little pink rose at the base is one of the old roses that

survived the nettles and rubbish which surrounded our garden when we first moved in. 'Maiden's Blush' a rampant grower sets lots of suckers which all come true. Another is 'Pink Chiffon'. *Nicotiana affinis* 'Lime Green', one white spiky dahlia, white sweet peas and lilies all so sweetly scented. Lilies are well worth growing but are a little disappointing in that they die out rather quickly, but there are varieties, like *L. candidum* and *L. x testaceum* which I would recommend to anyone as they really do increase. Sadly many of the beautiful De Graaff hybrids are not so good after two years or so. Many people grow these in tubs which I think is ideal, but for me it is just one more job that I never seem to get around to doing.

Then interspersed at the front is the fluffy, lime green flower *Alchemilla mollis*, which I use all summer and cannot think how I could do without it as it blends with every colour. It seeds freely so it enables one to give it away all the time. I always hope that everyone is going to enjoy it as much as I do.

For a summer buffet salmon is, I suppose, one of the luxuries and one which we will hardly ever be able to have again at the rate the price has risen in these last few years. There are many ways of cooking salmon but the best I have ever eaten was barbecued by an Indian tribe who live in one of the islands off Seattle. The magnificent fish were split like herring and spread open, then staked on slats of wood like chestnut fencing and cooked in front of open wood fires. It was fantastically good.

Cooking it the way Diana suggests is excellent and really does work with any size of cut, and I have found it very useful. I still prefer a plain mayonnaise though 'verte' does look most attractive. Another nice addition is to cube the cucumber and mix with a little yoghurt. Summer pudding is always a favourite and though it can be made with old-fashioned bread, it is good for a change made with sponge cakes.

When deciding on the menu for a summer buffet lunch, remember to keep the food light and easy to prepare, as one hopes the weather will be warm.

Pâté

25 g/1 oz/2 tablespoons butter
50 g/2 oz/$\frac{1}{3}$ cup onion, chopped
225 g/8 oz/1 cup chicken or turkey liver
pinch mixed herbs
1 clove garlic, crushed
salt and pepper
75 g/3 oz/$\frac{1}{3}$ cup butter
50 g/2 oz/$\frac{1}{4}$ cup cream cheese
1 tablespoon sherry
squeeze of lemon juice

Melt the 25 g/1 oz/2 tablespoons of butter, add the onion and soften, then add the chopped liver, herbs, garlic and seasoning and cook for about 3–4 minutes. Allow to cool then pass through a sieve. Cream the 75 g/3 oz/$\frac{1}{3}$ cup of butter and work in the sieved liver mixture, the cream cheese and the sherry, and a small squeeze of lemon juice. Check the seasoning and adjust if necessary. Put into a dish, smooth over the top, cover with clarified butter or a piece of cling film and put into the refrigerator. Serve the pâté with hot toast.

* This pâté freezes very well. Thaw overnight in the refrigerator.

Cold Salmon

The method given below is very easy and can be used for any size or cut of salmon.

1 salmon
1 sprig of parsley
1 bay leaf
8 peppercorns
1 tablespoon wine or cider vinegar
1 teaspoon salt

Wash and clean the fish. If a fish kettle is available put the fish on the tray and lower the tray into the kettle. If you do not have a kettle, use a large pan, and curl the fish round in the pan. Cover the fish with cold water, add the parsley, bay leaf, peppercorns, vinegar and salt. Bring it slowly to the boil, and let it boil for 3 minutes only. Take the pan off the heat and allow the fish to cool in the liquid.

(If the fish is to be served hot, leave it in the hot liquid for 10–15 minutes.)

Lift the fish out of the liquid, drain, and remove the skin, and lay on a serving dish.* Finely slice half a cucumber, and arrange the slices overlapping down the centre of the fish. Garnish with lettuce leaves, sliced tomato and some more sliced cucumber.

Instead of serving plain mayonnaise with the salmon, try this mayonnaise verte.

* The fish may be frozen at this stage, before any garnish is added.

Mayonnaise Verte

For the mayonnaise:
3 egg yolks
1 teaspoon french mustard
salt and freshly ground black pepper
1–2 tablespoons wine or cider vinegar
300 ml/½ pint/1¼ cups oil

40 g/1½ oz/1 cup spinach leaves
40 g/1½ oz/⅔ cup parsley, tarragon and chervil leaves
300 ml/½ pint/1¼ cups mayonnaise

Put the yolks in a basin with the mustard and a little salt and pepper, and beat well until thick. Then add the oil very slowly, beating well until the mixture is thick. Add a little of the vinegar to thin it down, then continue to add the oil beating well, and adding a little more vinegar when it gets thick again. When all the oil is added, add more vinegar to taste and adjust the seasoning.

Wash the spinach leaves, then blanch them by putting in boiling water, and boil with the herbs for 3 minutes, drain, rinse under cold water and squeeze dry. Pound or sieve the mixture, then add to the mayonnaise.

Summer Pudding

1 kg/2 lb/8 cups mixed fruit (We used gooseberries, black and redcurrants, and raspberries.)
100 g/4 oz/½ cup sugar
6–8 slices bread, crusts removed (not the pre-sliced type as it tends to make a rather soggy pudding)

Pick over the fruit, put into a pan with the sugar and cook until the fruit is tender, about 10–15 minutes. Meanwhile, cut two rounds of the bread to fit the top and bottom of a 900 ml/1½ pint/1 US quart bowl and line the bottom of the bowl with one of the slices. Line the sides of the bowl with the rest of the bread slices. Pour in the cooked fruit to nearly fill the bowl, keeping any surplus juice. Cover the fruit with the remaining round of bread and spoon over a little of the juice. Put a plate on top of the bowl, and place a 1 kg/2 lb weight on top. It is a good idea to stand the bowl on a plate in case some of the juice overflows. Leave in a cool place overnight.

Next day, remove the weight and the plate and turn the pudding out on to a serving dish. If any white bread still shows, spoon over a little more juice. Garnish with a few fresh raspberries.

This is very nice served with cream or a good cold egg custard.

Crème à la Vanille (sounds better than egg custard!)

300 ml/½ pint/1¼ cups milk
2 egg yolks
1 tablespoon caster sugar
1 teaspoon arrowroot
few drops vanilla essence

Bring the milk to boiling point. Meanwhile, cream the yolks, sugar, arrowroot and vanilla essence until thick then pour on the hot milk. Return to the rinsed-out pan and, stirring all the time, cook gently until the mixture coats the back of the spoon. Strain into a jug and allow to get cold.

Midsummer's Eve Party

One would hope for a lovely hot night for this party, at least allowing us to have drinks outside, but of course, in Britain, you can never be sure! My idea was to have shellfish and shell containers and a pyramid of flowers bursting from the shells to make a fountain of frothy pink flowers, delicate grasses and a touch of the seashore in the sea holly, *Eryngium giganteum*.

Visiting a lovely seaside house in Florida some years ago I was fascinated by the table decor which was made of different shells, so I thought I would like to pass the idea of a shell centrepiece on to you. This is how it was made.

Take a round silver cake board and before fixing your shells try laying them out the way they will look best and then arrange the shells to fit together. On this table I wanted a round arrangement as I thought that would look right, so I worked with that in mind. Should your table be long then I suggest the shells should be arranged in an oblong, tapering pattern which will fit your table better. You can still use the round board as oval boards are difficult to find. Just make your shells into an oblong pattern.

Get a small soup bowl or a round Oasis holder, in fact anything that will hold enough water for a few flowers, and fill this with damp Oasis. Stick this firmly down with 'Uhu' or a similar quick-drying glue. Take a packet of Polyfilla (or similar plaster filler), empty half into a bowl and mix with a little warm water until it is thoroughly wet but not runny. Make a mound of this up one side of the bowl, and start getting the shells pushed in firmly. Only do half at a time or one side, because once the paste dries it is impossible to move the shells if you happen to change your mind. I placed the larger shells to start with and then filled in with the smaller ones. If you should want to place these one on top of another, then put a little 'Uhu' on each shell and press them hard until they are really firm. Let this side dry off before you turn it round and decorate the other side.

This is really a fun thing to do for a summer party. If you think you might use it often then a little care must be taken in finishing it off, and I would strongly advise covering the base of the board with material so that it will not scratch the table if used continually.

Give all the flowers a good drink. They will need this because they will only be in damp Oasis and will flag unless they have first been in deep water for several hours. I like to have my flowers in water overnight if possible. If you want to arrange any of these table centres the day before, they will keep all right so long as you place the whole arrangement, vase and all, in a large polythene bag—the kind you get from the dry cleaners is best, but those supplied for rubbish collection will do very well. In this way you keep the air away from the flower heads so that they do not dehydrate and will come out as fresh and crisp as when they were first picked.

The foamy grass, *Lasiagrostis splendens*, is a plant that is definitely worth a mention and I would advise anyone to invest in a plant of this, as the delicate plumes are a delight in any vase. They are at their best in July being really open and fluffy. If caught at the right moment they will take up a solution of glycerine very well and stay fluffy and pretty all winter, but I have found it quite difficult to pick them at just the critical moment.

However, if you watch the plant really carefully, you may be able to pick them when they are fully open and then they are well worthwhile. My trouble has been that as soon as the plumes are ready it rains and they must be really dry before they are put into the solution. Despite all the difficulties, do try it!

Eryngium giganteum, perhaps better known to some as Miss Wilmott's Ghost is a sea holly and seemed so right for this arrangement. Its soft grey touch is ideal and tones down what could have been a rather sugary-pink arrangement. Once you get the first plant to thrive, then you have it for all time. *Astrantia major* and *Eryngium giganteum* are both worthy of a place in any garden. They seed freely and you will find you get some interesting cross pollinations especially if you grow the pink astrantia as well.

The larger pale pink rose is one of David Austin's, 'The Prioress', delicate soft pink, enchanting. It was hybridized from 'Constance Spry' but flowers twice in the year. On the far left is 'New Dawn', a delicate pink rose which flowers a little later than the others and will climb and scramble up an old apple tree in no time at all. It has a long flowering period and one can pick this rose right through August.

At the lower front are the old-fashioned shrub roses 'Maiden's Blush'. These flat-headed roses, sweetly scented, are a dream for a flower arranger, though sadly, they only last for two days. They were in the garden when we bought the house and I have come to love them dearly.

The pink tobacco plant, or *Nicotiana*, is a seedling which arrived in a packet of seeds two years ago and we have grown it on. It has such a lovely soft pink back to a white trumpet.

If the weather is hot, one does not always want a lot of 'heavy' food which is why we chose fish for midsummer's eve. All the dishes are fairly straightforward to make. The crab, perhaps, is the most fiddly to prepare but, I think, well worth the effort.

Fish Mousse

450 g/1 lb fresh haddock or cod fillet
salt
8 peppercorns
juice of half a lemon
300 ml/½ pint/1¼ cups milk
1 bay leaf
sprig of parsley
30 g/1 oz/2 tablespoons butter
1 teaspoon paprika pepper
20 g/¾ oz/2 tablespoons flour
7.5 g/¼ oz/½ packet gelatine
3 tablespoons double cream
1 egg white

First of all cook the fish. Wash the fillet, skin it and put into a buttered fireproof dish with the salt, 4 peppercorns and the lemon juice. Cover with a piece of buttered paper and place in a preheated oven 180°C/350°F/Gas Mark 4, for 15 minutes. Allow to cool.

Put the milk into a pan with the bay leaf, 4 peppercorns and the parsley over a gentle heat and leave to infuse, then strain. Melt the butter in a clean saucepan, add the paprika and cook for a few seconds, take off the heat and add the flour and blend well. Pour on the flavoured milk, return to the heat and bring to the boil, stirring all the time. Pour into a bowl, cover with a piece of damp greaseproof paper and leave it to cool.

Strain the fish, flake it, making sure there are no bones left in, then pound it. If a pestle and mortar are not available a round-ended rolling pin and a basin will serve the purpose.

Add the cold sauce gradually. Soak the gelatine in 4 tablespoons of cold water, then dissolve over gentle heat and stir into the fish mixture. Whip the cream lightly, and whisk the egg white and fold these into the mixture. Turn the mousse into a lightly-oiled 900 ml/1½ pint/1 US quart mould and leave to set.*

Turn the mousse out on to a serving plate and decorate with slices of tomato and cucumber twirls.

* Freeze at this stage.

Prawns Sicilienne

175 g/6 oz/1 cup long grain rice
50 g/2 oz/½ cup almonds
salt and pepper
2–3 tablespoons french dressing

For the sauce:
150 ml/¼ pint/generous ½ cup thick, bland mayonnaise
juice of 1 orange
juice of 1 lemon
few drops Tabasco sauce
1 shallot, finely chopped
small can tomato purée
100 g/4 oz prawns (shelled)
a few whole fresh prawns for garnish

First of all cook the rice in plenty of boiling salted water until just cooked, drain, rinse well with cold water and leave to get cold. Pour boiling water on to the almonds, leave for a few minutes then slip off the skins. Cut them into shreds and add them to the rice with the french dressing. Season well, put into an oiled ring mould and set on one side.

Now make the sauce. Mix the mayonnaise, the orange and lemon juices, the Tabasco sauce, shallot, tomato purée and blend well, adjusting the seasoning. Add the prawns. Turn the rice out of the mould on to a serving plate and pour the sauce into the middle. Garnish with whole fresh prawns.

Dressed Crab

Crabs, like all shellfish, must be fresh and feel heavy for their size. If you feel nervous about removing the stomach and the gills, your fishmonger will remove them for you.

1 boiled crab
2 tablespoons dried breadcrumbs
1 tablespoon cream
salt and freshly ground pepper
1 hard-boiled egg
1 dessertspoon chopped parsley

First of all remove the big claws and the legs. Then hold the shell in one hand, put two fingers of the other hand into the hole left by the claws and pull the shell apart from the body. Then remove the stomach—the small sac which lies behind the eyes—and the gills, these are sometimes called dead men's fingers, which lie around the big shell. Throw both these away. Also, if there is any green meat in the big shell, throw it away.

Scrape the brown meat from inside the shell and put into a basin. Crack the claws, using a weight, and put all the white meat from them into another basin. Remove as much meat as possible from the body. This is the fiddly bit! You may find using a skewer helpful. Leave the white meat on one side.

Break off the sides of the shell, you will notice a line going round the edge—use this as a guide, then wash and dry it well.

Cream the brown meat, add the breadcrumbs and enough cream to moisten the mixture and season thoroughly. Arrange this meat across the centre of the shell, and the white meat on either side of it.*

Sieve the egg yolk, chop the white. Decorate the crab with stripes of egg yolk, egg white and the chopped parsley. Arrange the shell on some lettuce leaves and decorate with the legs.

* Freeze at this stage for a maximum of one month.

Plaice in Scallop Shells

This is the only hot dish for this party—we thought it would have 'warm' appeal! You will need four scallop shells to serve the plaice in an attractive way.

4 whole plaice fillets
100 g/4 oz mushrooms
salt and pepper
150 ml/¼ pint/generous ½ cup white sauce, fairly thick
creamed potatoes (made from 1 kg/2 lb potatoes)
15 g/½ oz/1 tablespoon butter

Skin the plaice fillets, and wipe with a damp cloth. Wipe the mushrooms and cut 12 slices from the largest or the best shaped and put these on one side for garnishing. Chop the rest of them, and cook lightly in a little butter. Season with salt and pepper.

Lay the plaice fillets, skin side up on a board and spread the mushroom mixture on the middle, fold in the ends, enclosing the mushroom mixture and place them in the buttered scallop shells. Spoon over the sauce, then fill a piping bag fitted with a large vegetable rose pipe, pipe a ring of potato round the edge of the shells. Cook the mushroom slices in the butter and arrange 3 slices, overlapping on each shell. Put the shells on to a baking tray and bake in the oven, 200°C/400°F/Gas Mark 6 for 20 minutes.

* This dish can easily be prepared beforehand and frozen, but allow an extra 30 minutes cooking time if reheating from frozen.

Barbecue (illustration page 41)

A barbecue is one of the most informal ways of entertaining and is entirely dependent on the weather, which is why it is so useful in places like Australia and California where in summer you can rely on having a rain-free season. In Britain, of course, it is quite different. As these things have to be arranged ahead one simply has to take a chance. If it rains you can, of course, move everything into a garage or outhouse for cooking, but then you really have to eat in the house as the smoke under cover makes it almost impossible to eat where the food is being cooked. So always clear the garage or some covered area for such an emergency and have enough chairs around for everyone to sit wherever you finally land up. But let's hope for a fine day.

As the men mostly like to look after the barbecue that's great as they take care of the cooking, and all the hostess has to worry about is having the food prepared, or marinated where necessary, and making salads of various kinds.

Out of doors it is best to avoid flowers in water, or cut flowers generally, as these tend to wilt very quickly when exposed to open air. Make use of pot plants which can be arranged in a basket or used as a pot-et-fleur together with some cut flowers placed in a small soup bowl in wet Oasis and incorporated in the foliage of the plants. It gives the added colour which is pretty for a party, yet you still have the plants which will make an attractive and long-lasting arrangement for later. The plants can be arranged in a basket lined with foil and covered with a layer of moss to conceal the pots. I think they last a little better this way. But they can look lovely unpotted, too. Just fill a plastic dish with soil. Plant it up with the taller subjects at the back, coming to smaller plants in front and put in the basket. This gives you a planted garden which can be used for weeks in the house once the party is over.

Here I have used a collection of mixed vegetables because they are so decorative and one doesn't often get the chance to use them, as vegetables indoors are sometimes regarded as gimmicky. The soup tureen was built up with a high block of Oasis, soaked, so that it was ready for the stems of cut flowers. As you will see in the photograph, it is mainly vegetables: green tomatoes, onion, cauliflower, calabrese, carrots, heads of globe artichokes, all of which can be removed and eaten in due course. The shades of green were many and so varied that I felt it a pity to add any strong colour, so the touch of pink from the rich and rare passion flower was all that was needed. The stem of Bells of Ireland, *Molucella laevis*, gave the required height and line for the top of the arrangement. To make the cauliflower sit quite firmly I inserted a thick piece of stick in the stalk of the cauliflower and through into the Oasis. It is a simple arrangement, suitable to the occasion with nothing to flag save the marrow leaves. These I found quite by chance as I walked round the garden the day before so I picked them, put the stems immediately into boiling water for one minute and then completely submerged them in a bucket of water overnight and they lasted for days. I must add here that this would not be possible early in the season as they are much too tender then. The giant onion was one of the small ones grown at Clack's Farm and weighed exactly 680 grammes/1½ lb!

The table could be laid with a hessian or burlap cloth though coarse linen in green or fawn is perhaps the most effective with wooden bowls for mixed salads, baskets for crisp fresh bread and copper bowls of colourful fruit. Fruit is of course, equally as decorative as vegetables but here I felt the vegetables were a little more unusual.

Simplicity is the keynote and the rustic appearance is in keeping with the occasion. Even when eating out of doors in an informal way it is rewarding to make the presentation as attractive as possible.

The food can be prepared during the day. If some of the meat is to be marinated it is left in the marinade in the morning. Before cooking can begin, the barbecue must be prepared, the charcoal heated in advance. If the charcoal is not hot enough, the food will take longer to cook, and your guests will get very hungry! Barbecue food is best kept very simple.

For this barbecue we chose to cook lamb chops, hamburgers, two different kebabs, sausages (which are not in the photograph) with tomatoes and a crunchy salad. Potatoes in their jackets would take rather a long time to cook over the grill, so they are cooked indoors in the oven, already wrapped in foil, then they can be kept hot on the grill. Instead of, or as well as, potatoes, you could serve soft rolls or baps with the barbecue.

Hamburgers

450 g/1 lb minced beef
4 tablespoons fresh breadcrumbs
pinch of mixed herbs
salt and freshly ground black pepper
1 egg to mix (size 6/small)

Mince the meat again then mix well with the breadcrumbs, herbs, salt and pepper. Then add enough of the beaten egg to bind it all together. Divide the mixture into six equal pieces and shape into flattish rounds in your hands. These will take about 4–5 minutes each side to cook on the grill. The quantities given will make 6 hamburgers.

Lamb Chops

6 cutlets or loin chops

Sweet and sour baste:
2 tablespoons soy sauce
1 tablespoon syrup or honey

Trim the chops and scrape off a little of the fat and meat at the end of the bone to make it easier to hold. Combine the soy sauce and syrup or honey and brush the mixture over the chops and, if possible, leave to marinate for at least an hour or so before grilling—10–15 minutes on each side.

Sausages

Chipolatas are the best sausages for barbecueing as they do not take too long to cook. Grill for about 10–15 minutes.

Lamb's Liver, Mushroom and Tomato Kebabs

6 tomatoes
225 g/$\frac{1}{2}$ lb lamb's liver
225 g/$\frac{1}{2}$ lb mushrooms, medium-sized caps

Barbecue baste:
3 tablespoons tomato ketchup
3 tablespoons cooking oil
pinch of herbs

Cut the tomatoes in half and thread one half on to each of three skewers. Cut the liver into even-sized pieces, and take the stalks off the mushrooms. Thread the pieces of liver on to the skewers alternately with the mushrooms, when the skewer is filled, finish with the other halves of tomato. Brush with the barbecue baste and leave to marinate for an hour or so before grilling for about 10 minutes on each side.

Lamb Kebabs

Marinade:
2 tablespoons oil
1 tablespoon vinegar
1 small clove garlic
salt and pepper

350 g/$\frac{3}{4}$ lb lean lamb
12 small onions
1 green pepper

Mix together the oil and vinegar, and add the crushed clove of garlic with the salt and pepper to make the marinade. Cut the lamb into pieces and leave it to marinate for several hours or overnight if possible.

Peel the onions and de-seed the pepper (cut round the stalk, pull it out, then shake out the seeds) and cut into strips. Thread the lamb, pepper and onions on to three skewers, then grill for 10 minutes on each side.

Barbecue Sauce

150 ml/$\frac{1}{4}$ pint/generous $\frac{1}{2}$ cup dry white wine
150 ml/$\frac{1}{4}$ pint/generous $\frac{1}{2}$ cup stock
4 tablespoons/$\frac{1}{4}$ cup oil
15 g/$\frac{1}{2}$ oz/1 tablespoon butter
1 medium onion, finely chopped

1 clove garlic, crushed
salt
large pinch paprika pepper
2 teaspoons chopped herbs

Mix all the ingredients in a pan, bring to the boil and simmer for about 30 minutes.

Crispy Salad

$\frac{1}{2}$ red cabbage
$\frac{1}{2}$ white cabbage

2 eating apples
salted peanuts

Cut the halves of cabbage in two and remove the core, then shred very finely, keeping the red and white cabbages separate. Arrange the red cabbage on one side of a salad bowl, the white cabbage on the other side. Sprinkle over some salted peanuts and arrange the cored and thinly sliced apple on top.

The Children's Party (illustration page 48)

Children love an air of mystery, and something a little special, they are almost born with an air of one-upmanship! So it is a great thrill to give a party that is a little different from those they normally attend. A picnic is always exciting, so my daughter had the idea of filling individual shoe boxes with a selection of food which could be taken off and eaten just where they liked, no formality, no sitting for a long time in one place, and it proved to be a great success. The shoe boxes were easily come by, any shoe shop seems to have an abundance of empty boxes, so that proved to be much simpler to deal with than I had imagined. The boxes were covered with some left-over Christmas paper and tied with a flowered ribbon, though it could be done with anything of your choice. The highlight of the food was undoubtedly the individual iced sponge cakes which had each child's name on. Nowadays, savoury things seem to have replaced many of the sweeter kinds of foods. So sausages on sticks, sausage rolls, cheese straws, savoury sandwiches, potato crisps and so on, seem to go down very well. Chocolate biscuits and birthday cake are expected, of course, if it is a birthday party.

I have asked Diana to include our famous rainbow cake recipe, as no one in our family could have a birthday without it. It is made up of two tiers of white and two of pink sponge, sandwiched together with layers of icing and covered completely with white icing. For us, we had to have our names on top picked out in silver balls! It is funny how these things stick in one's mind and children love being part of this sort of tradition. I have seen lovely cakes made like Dougal of television fame and as a shoe for the old lady who lived in a shoe. A good basic sponge mixture, a lot of imagination, and lots of different size cake tins make all this possible. The cottage-type house is very effective and is made of two oblong sponge cakes, with a third split to form a slanting roof and attached with cocktail sticks. Covered with a layer of icing and decorated with coloured chocolate buttons it is very effective indeed. (In fact, sweets are an ideal decoration for making eyes, mouths, etc.) Chocolate icing covered the house, with white for the windows and green for the door.

For this out-of-doors party I tried to think of a decoration which would be fun for the table and which would not blow over or wilt in the heat, hence the idea of the lollipop tree. It serves a dual purpose as it can be eaten afterwards. Find a well-shaped, substantial branch of either fruit wood or oak—those stiff, knobbly branches seem to be the most effective. Place the branch in a mound of wet Plaster of Paris, which I use as it sets so quickly that you can just stand and hold the branch in place until the plaster is set hard. Wire the lollipops on to the tree with firm florist's wires. Take the end of a strip of crêpe paper about 2–3 cm/1 in wide and bind round the branch to cover the wire, using a touch of glue to keep it in place. Make your ribbon bows so that they cover the paper. The little figures were made from a packet of Liquorice Allsorts; make the arms and legs first by threading the sweets on to the cocktail stick, then make the head and body in the same way and attach them all together, pushing them firmly into the body. For some reason a few did not hold together so I used a little clear plastic cement—which was a pity as they could not be eaten later!

Another idea for a tree is to make it out of boiled sweets and toffees, on the same lines as the fruit tree for the Hallowe'en party. Make a dunce's cap from small mesh wire netting, rolling it round into a cone, and then cutting the bottom off straight. Fill with old pieces of crushed Oasis. Wire each toffee or sweet by taking a florist's wire, bend it like a hair pin, place the rounded end over the tufted end of the toffee paper bringing one wire round it and the second wire, and this will make a stalk which you can push into the cone. One sweet sticks out at the top, the others making circles round the cone. Make rings of different colours for the best effect, with as brightly-coloured sweets as possible. Then attach one or two ribbon bows to add more colour. Put a thick stick up the cone into the Oasis and the other end of the stick into a small flower pot which you have filled with wet Plaster of Paris. Hold it firmly for a few minutes until it has set.

Another nice idea is to have a birthday chair and to decorate it with a small bunch of flowers tied on to the back. This has been done in our family to my knowledge for five generations and gives enormous pleasure.

The Sandwiches–Suggested Fillings

Although most children seem to prefer white bread, make the sandwiches with both brown and white bread. Apart from the usual yeast extract (Marmite) and jam fillings try—

cheese and chutney
sardine—mash the sardines, season with freshly-ground black pepper, and decorate with some slices of cucumber
cream cheese with finely chopped pineapple
chocolate spread sprinkled with some chopped nuts

Sausages on Sticks

These are always very popular, so have plenty!

Take some chipolata sausages and if they are very long, twist them in half before cutting them. Fry them or cook them in the oven—I think this last method is the easiest for cooking a large quantity. Melt a little fat in a roasting tin, and cook the sausages at 200°C/400°F/Gas Mark 6 for about 25 minutes. Drain well on kitchen paper and put a cocktail stick in each.

Rainbow Cake

175 g/6 oz/¾ cup butter
350 g/12 oz/1½ cups sugar
4 eggs
250 ml/8 fl oz/1 cup milk
350 g/12 oz/3 cups self-raising flour
3 teaspoons baking powder
cochineal

Beat butter and sugar to a cream. Separate eggs, add yolks to the butter and sugar and beat hard for five minutes. Mix whites with the milk, sift flour with baking powder and gradually add all to the mixture, beating hard all the time. Pour half the mixture into two prepared sandwich tins 18 cm/7 in in diameter. Add cochineal to the remaining mixture and pour into two more tins. Bake at 200°C/400°F/Gas Mark 6 for 20 minutes or until firm to the touch.

Below are two recipes for icing the rainbow cake—the traditional version and American frosting.

Icing:
450 g/1 lb/4 cups icing sugar
water
squeeze of lemon juice

Sift the icing sugar and add enough water to make a firm consistency and sandwich the cakes with some of this.

Dilute the remaining icing with more water and a squeeze of lemon juice to make a coating consistency and pour over the cake and let it run down the sides helping it with a palette knife. To prevent bringing crumbs from the cake into the icing keep the knife on the icing until the cake is covered.

Leave to set, then using coloured or silver balls spell out the name of the birthday child on top.

American frosting:
300 g/10 oz/1½ cups granulated sugar
4 tablespoons water
2 egg whites
¼ teaspoon cream of tartar

Put all the ingredients into a bowl and suspend over a pan half-filled with gently boiling water. Stir the mixture in the bowl for about 10 minutes or until every grain of sugar has dissolved—this is very important otherwise the icing will not be smooth. Beat the mixture using a rotary or hand electric beater (still keeping the bowl over the boiling water) until it thickens. When it becomes too stiff for the rotary beater use a wire balloon whisk. When the mixture leaves a good trail over the surface, remove the bowl from the pan of water and beat for a further minute or two.

Sandwich the cakes with some of this icing and spread the remainder over the top and sides of the cake. This icing does not smooth as easily over the surface of the cake as the earlier recipe.

Andrew
Sandy
Anne
Jane
Peter
John
Mary
Diana

The Named Cake

100 g/4 oz/½ cup soft margarine
100 g/4 oz/½ cup caster sugar
2 eggs (size 3/large)
175 g/6 oz/1½ cups self-raising flour
2 tablespoons milk

Icing:
450 g/1 lb/3½ cups icing sugar
water to mix
yellow food colouring
cocoa powder

Cut a piece of greaseproof paper to fit the bottom of a Swiss roll tin 30 × 20 cm/12 × 8 in, brush the tin with melted fat, lay in the paper and grease it also. Preheat the oven to 190°C/375°F/Gas Mark 5.

Put all the ingredients into a mixing bowl and beat well for one minute but for under a minute if using an electric mixer. Pour the mixture into the prepared tin, and spread it evenly, hollowing the centre slightly and bake it for 25–30 minutes. Turn out on to a wire rack to cool.*

To make the icing, sift the sugar into a bowl and add enough water to make a thick coating consistency. Add the food colouring. Pour the icing on to the cake, leaving enough for writing the names later, and spread it over the surface. Put the remaining icing into a basin and cover with a lid. Cut the cake into slices before the icing sets.

Mix the cocoa powder into the remaining icing to make a good colour. Fill a piping bag, fitted with a no. 2 writing nozzle, with the chocolate icing and write the name of a child on each slice of cake.

* Freeze at this stage.

Crispy Lemon Cake

100 g/4 oz/½ cup butter or margarine
100 g/4 oz/½ cup caster sugar
1 egg
100 g/4 oz/1 cup self-raising flour

Topping:
juice of 1 lemon
75 g/3 oz/⅓ cup caster sugar

Grease and line with greaseproof paper a sandwich tin 20 cm/8 in in diameter. Soften the butter without letting it 'oil', beat in the sugar then add the beaten egg, and stir in the sifted flour. Turn into the prepared tin and bake at 190°C/375°F/Gas Mark 5 for 15 minutes, then reduce the heat to 180°C/350°F/Gas Mark 4 for a further 10 minutes. For the topping, mix together the lemon juice and sugar. When the cake is cooked, turn it out on to a wire rack and while it is still hot spoon over the topping. The juice soaks into the cake and the sugar makes the crispy topping.

Malt Fruit Loaf

350 g/12 oz/3 cups plain flour
½ teaspoon bicarbonate of soda
1 teaspoon baking powder
4 tablespoons golden syrup
4 tablespoons malt extract
25 g/1 oz/2 tablespoons demerara sugar
2 eggs
150 ml/¼ pint/generous ½ cup milk
250 g/9 oz/1¾ cups sultanas, raisins or dates

Grease a loaf tin measuring 23 × 13 × 7 cm/9 × 5 × 2⅜ in. Preheat oven to 150°C/300°F/Gas Mark 2.

Sift the flour with the bicarbonate of soda and baking powder. Melt the syrup, malt extract and sugar over a gentle heat. Beat the eggs and add the milk. Pour the melted mixture into the flour with the egg and milk, add the fruit and mix them all together. Pour into prepared tin and bake for about 1½ hours. Turn on to a wire rack to cool. Wrap in foil and leave several days to mature.*

The loaf can be served either plain or buttered.

* This loaf freezes well.

Melting Moment Biscuits

75 g/3 oz/⅜ cup butter
75 g/3 oz/⅜ cup lard or shortening
150 g/5 oz/¾ cup caster sugar
1 egg
few drops vanilla essence
300 g/10 oz/2½ cups self-raising flour
50 g/2 oz/2 cups cornflakes, lightly crushed
glacé cherries

Switch oven to 200°C/400°F/Gas Mark 6.

Cream the butter and the shortening together, then add the sugar and cream until light. Add the beaten egg and vanilla essence then mix in the sifted flour. Divide the mixture into balls about the size of a walnut and roll in the cornflakes. Place on a greased baking tray, and flatten slightly with the back of a wooden spoon. Place a halved glacé cherry in the centre, and bake for about 15–20 minutes. Cool on a wire tray. The quantities given will make about 30 biscuits.

Chocolate Crunchies

50 g/2 oz/¼ cup butter
50 g/2 oz/⅓ cup icing sugar
2 tablespoons golden syrup
3 tablespoons cocoa powder
75 g/3 oz/3½ cups Rice Krispies

Melt the butter, sugar, syrup and cocoa powder in a pan without allowing it to boil. Stir in the Rice Krispies and mix well. Spoon into paper cases and leave to set. This makes about 18 crunchies.

Priory Biscuits

100 g/4 oz/1 cup plain flour
½ teaspoon baking powder
large pinch salt
large pinch cream of tartar
100 g/4 oz/½ cup butter
100 g/4 oz/½ cup sugar
100 g/4 oz/1½ cups rolled oats
1 teaspoon bicarbonate of soda
1 dessertspoon hot water
2 tablespoons golden syrup

Sift the flour, baking powder, salt and cream of tartar together. Beat the butter until soft, beat in the sugar and stir in the rolled oats. Dissolve the bicarbonate of soda in the hot water, warm the syrup and add them to the mixture with the flour. Leave the mixture to stand for about 20 minutes then put out in teaspoonfuls on to greased baking trays, allowing space for them to spread during cooking, and bake at 180°C/350°F/Gas Mark 4 for about 10 minutes. Put on a wire rack to cool. This makes about 30 biscuits.

The following recipe for a chocolate cake is sweetened with syrup instead of sugar; this makes it a slightly sticky cake which is part of its attraction.

Chocolate Sandwich Cake

4 tablespoons boiling water
2 teaspoons instant coffee powder
100 g/4 oz/½ cup butter
2 tablespoons golden syrup
75 g/3 oz/½ cup sweetened chocolate powder
2 eggs
150 g/5 oz/1¼ cups self-raising flour
1 dessertspoon cocoa powder

Grease 2 sandwich tins, 18 cm/7 in in diameter, line them with a disc of greaseproof paper to fit and grease the paper also.

Pour the boiling water on to the coffee powder and leave it to cool.

Cream the butter until it is soft then add the syrup and the chocolate powder, beating the mixture well. Separate the eggs and beat the yolks into the mixture. Sift the flour with the cocoa powder and add it to the mixture with the coffee. Whip the egg whites, not too stiffly, and fold into the mixture. Divide between the two tins, smooth the top and bake at 190°C/375°F/Gas Mark 5 for 20 minutes. Turn the cakes on to a wire rack to cool.

When they are cold sandwich them together with either jam, or a butter icing made by creaming 50 g/2 oz/¼ cup butter with 100 g/4 oz/¾ cup icing sugar, a tablespoon of top of the milk and chocolate powder to taste.

The Wedding Reception (illustration page 54)

A wedding is for all of us a happy and exciting occasion. Where to hold the reception is always a problem usually solved by the season of the year. Many brides feel they would like to have it at home if at all possible, and for spring and summer the marquee in the garden would be ideal. I well remember a friend of mine with four daughters who always wished he had bought the marquee after the first wedding! Nevertheless, whether the reception is held at home or in an hotel or hall, flowers will play an important part. But they will play an even more important role in the church, and I recommend strongly that more should be spent on the flowers for the church than on those for the reception. People sit in church and have little else to do before a wedding but study the flowers. At the reception the key point is the entrance—this should be made welcoming and pretty, as the first impression is the one that counts. After that everyone is meeting with friends, talking about the wedding generally, food and drink take over and the flowers take second place. It is also advisable to have a good arrangement near to where the bride will be receiving the guests.

My advice about food is that it should be fresh and appetizing, there should not be too many varieties and that you should see everything can be eaten easily in the hand. It is easy to forget that many guests travel a long way and are usually quite hungry. As you will see from the photograph, Diana really makes excellent bouchées with different fillings, freshly-cut sandwiches, asparagus rolls, scampi and piquant sauce all quite a good size. The coffee meringues are delicious for those with a sweet tooth.

The two-tier wedding cake is beautifully iced and has a top-knot of flowers and a garland around the base. This garland is made on a piece of thick string and the unwired flowers are bound on to it with a fine silver wire. As it does not have to last very long it is safe enough not to wire each individual flower, but it must be kept in a plastic bag out of the air until the very last minute. To make the top-knot, which I prefer to the usual silver vase, I take a small piece of wet Oasis and cover it with kitchen foil, into which the firm-stemmed flowers go quite easily but one or two of the more fragile flowers may need a small piece of florist's wire to support the stems.

Buffet flowers need to be kept high and out of the way of the food and those who serve it. This two-tier vase is ideal, and two or more can be used according to the number of people and the length of the buffet. We chose pink and white for the wedding and it is nice, if possible, to link the colouring right through from the colour of the wedding dress and the bridesmaids' dresses to the church flowers and the reception. The thin buffet cloth was underlined in pink (with a sheet actually!). Though I did not drape the cloth with a Victorian fern garland this can be done and makes quite a nice finish; the garland is simply attached to the cloth with dressmaking pins. The flowers chosen for the two-tier vase were branches of sweetly scented lime flowers with all the outside leaves removed, and sprays of the lovely lime-green *Alchemilla mollis*, which gives the delicate outline for the heavier flowers. For these some stems of *Lilium regale*, a foxglove, side shoots of the beautiful white delphinium, white sprays of anthemis, the white floribunda rose 'Iceberg' and the delicious soft-pink rose 'Chaucer'. What a delight this rose is—it is a sport of 'Constance Spry' hybridized by David Austin—with all the qualities of 'Constance Spry' and the additional attribute of flowering twice yearly. I think the value of the delicate background material is well emphasized here.

A special table for the cake is often provided and this can be raised on a dais so that the cake-cutting ceremony can be seen by everyone. If you have the opportunity to make a special cloth for the cake table, one of the prettiest I ever saw was made with layers of tulle and it looked delightful. These cloths have to be made on the cross and circular so that they require a great deal of material but can be made very effectively from inexpensive butter muslin. The effect is completed by garlanding with green fern caught up with a posy of rosebuds and a few smaller flowers. These little touches really make such a difference to the overall appearance. For the marquee itself nothing looks better than hanging baskets, as these attract attention away from the poles. The look of the poles can be improved by the use of Oasis which is covered with a layer of kitchen foil and then a layer of wire netting. Two of these should be fixed on each side of the poles, so that the flowers spill over giving the effect of a ring, with plenty of flowers and sprays hanging gracefully down.

A pedestal arrangement is ideal should the reception be held in the house or hall, and flowers raised in this way are easily seen by everyone. Flowers for a pedestal need to be carefully chosen; good tall light foliage for the height, either flowering tree or shrub blossom in spring, like cherry, azalea or apple blossom, branches of stripped lime flowers in summer, autumnal-coloured foliage in October and bare branches of lichen in winter. (These latter are often the most difficult to obtain.) Then some large bold flowers concentrated in the centre of the arrangement, such as open roses, dahlias, hydrangea heads, large poppies and something tall and spiky to form the background. It is always better to do one really dramatic arrangement than too many small ones, and strategically placed it is all that is needed. Pedestals arranged in a marquee cause difficulties on occasion as the sloping sides may not give enough room to display the pedestal's height in its correct proportions.

When the engagement is announced and the wedding day has been fixed, one of the first things to do is to make the wedding cake. As most people know, a fruit cake improves with keeping before the almond paste, icing and decoration is put on. After the wedding, it is traditional to keep the top tier as the couple's first child's Christening cake. Cover the top and sides well with clean greaseproof paper, put it into a *firm* container, seal the edges and store it carefully in a corner of your freezer. It must be in a firm container, otherwise it will collapse under the weight of other items in the freezer, and the cake will be damaged. Allow about two days for it to thaw completely. Do not leave it until the last minute before taking out, in case it has suffered any damage which may need to be repaired.

The bouchée cases can be made about two weeks before the day and stored in a tin. The sandwiches, except the egg and watercress and the cucumber and mint, can also be made ahead and frozen.

Wedding Cake

For the two cakes:
1 kg/$2\frac{1}{2}$ lb/5 cups mixed dried fruit
100 g/4 oz/$\frac{1}{2}$ cup glacé cherries
150 ml/$\frac{1}{4}$ pint/generous $\frac{1}{2}$ cup brandy, sherry or fruit juice
50 g/2 oz/$\frac{1}{3}$ cup whole almonds
575 g/19 oz/$4\frac{3}{4}$ cups plain flour
pinch of salt
$1\frac{1}{2}$ teaspoons cinnamon
$1\frac{1}{2}$ teaspoons nutmeg
$1\frac{1}{2}$ tablespoons cocoa powder
50 g/2 oz/$\frac{1}{2}$ cup ground almonds
375 g/13 oz/$1\frac{1}{2}$ cups unsalted butter
375 g/13 oz/$1\frac{1}{2}$ cups caster sugar
2 lemons
1 orange
3 teaspoons black treacle
7 eggs (size 2–3/large)

Wash, if necessary, the dried fruit and check through to make sure there are no bits of stalk and place in a bowl. Wash, dry well and quarter the glacé cherries and add to the dried fruit. Pour on the brandy, sherry or fruit juice and leave to soak overnight.

Brush 2 round cake tins, one 15 cm/6 in and one 23 cm/9 in in diameter with a little melted fat and line the sides and bottoms with double greaseproof paper, lightly greasing this also.

Skin the almonds by pouring boiling water over them and leave for about 3 minutes, drain and the skins will come off easily. Then chop them and add to the soaked fruit. Sift the flour with the salt, spices and cocoa powder and then add the ground almonds. Beat the butter to a soft cream, add the sugar and the grated rinds of the lemons and orange and cream until light and fluffy, then beat in the treacle. Beat the eggs and add gradually into the creamed mixture, beating well between each addition. Stir in the dried fruit alternately with the flour, and mix well.

Divide the mixture between the two tins, making the bigger cake very slightly deeper than the small one. Smooth the tops and hollow out the centres of the cakes so that they will bake flat.

Bake the cakes in the centre of the oven at 150°C/300°F/Gas Mark 2 for 2 to $2\frac{1}{2}$ hours for the 15 cm/6 in cake and $3\frac{1}{2}$ to 4 hours for the 23 cm/9 in cake. To test if they are cooked, push a warmed skewer or knitting needle into the centre of the cake and if it comes out clean the cake is cooked. Leave the cakes to cool in their tins.

To store the cakes before icing them, sprinkle the tops with a little extra brandy, wrap in greaseproof paper and foil and leave in a cool place until needed.

Almond paste for both cakes:
475 g/17 oz/4 cups icing sugar
475 g/17 oz/$2\frac{1}{4}$ cups caster sugar
475 g/17 oz/4 cups ground almonds
7 egg yolks (keep the whites for the icing)
1 tablespoon sherry
3 drops almond essence
3 drops vanilla essence

You will also need:
450 g/1 lb apricot jam, melted and sieved
piece of string
ruler

Sift the icing sugar into a bowl, add the caster sugar and the ground almonds and mix them all well together. Make a well in the centre and into it put the yolks, sherry and the essences and stir all together, then knead to make a firm paste. Keep the almond paste in a plastic bag to prevent it from drying out.

To almond ice the cakes take two-thirds of the almond paste, keeping the rest in the plastic bag, and start with the bigger cake.

Roll out about half of the paste to make a round to fit the top of the cake, using the tin the cake was baked in as a guide. Turn the cake upside down and brush with the sieved apricot jam, and place the round of almond paste on to it. Roll the other half of the almond paste with the trimmings from the top into a long roll to fit round the sides of the cake. To measure this, take a piece of string, place round the circumference and cut the string to the size. Measure the depth of the cake with the ruler and flatten the roll with a rolling pin and cut it to the size required. Brush the sides of the cake with the sieved apricot jam, lay the cake on its side on the almond paste and roll the paste on to it. Press it into the cake well, and smooth over the joins. Almond paste the other cake in the same way and leave them in a cool place for a week to dry before putting on the royal icing.

Royal icing for both cakes:
5 egg whites
1½ teaspoons glycerine
3 teaspoons lemon juice
1.5 kg/ 3 lb icing sugar, sifted
straight edge or ruler at least 38 cm/ 15 in long.

Beat the egg whites, glycerine and lemon juice together and gradually beat in the icing sugar. This can be done in an electric mixer at the slowest speed. Continue to beat it until it will just stand in peaks and is a coating consistency. If using the electric beater be careful not to over-beat it. Put the icing into an airtight container and leave overnight, to allow some of the air bubbles to disperse.

Put a little icing in the middle of two silver cake boards 20 cm/8 in and 28 cm/11 in in diameter and put the cakes on to them. Put more icing, about 6 tablespoonfuls for the larger cake, on to its top and smooth with the ruler, going backwards and forwards until the top is smooth.

Never leave the icing in the bowl uncovered otherwise it will get a skin on it, so while you are icing, keep it covered with a damp cloth.

Place the cake on a turntable, or if one is not available, use an upturned pudding basin. With a palette knife, spread the surplus icing from the top down the sides of the cake and add a little more, spreading the icing evenly round the sides of the cake. Use a plastic spatula with a straight edge at an angle of 45° against the icing, turn the cake round, keeping the spatula still and smooth the sides of the cake.

Ice the other cake in the same way. Next day, scrape off any bumps with a knife before putting on a thin second coat of icing. Leave the cakes in an airy place to dry for about a week before decorating them. Put any remaining icing into a covered container.

Decoration

If you are inexperienced in icing it is far better to keep the design simple. For practice in working with an icing bag, use mashed potato in a large piping bag fitted with a large rose pipe and pipe rosettes etc. on a plastic top. To make your own icing bag (and you will need several), take a piece of greaseproof paper 25 cm/10 in square and fold it in half diagonally. Roll it into a cone with a nice sharp point and turn over and tuck down the projecting 'flaps' to secure the bag. Cut off the point and drop in the desired pipe—for the scrolls a scroll pipe is needed. Generously half-fill the bag with icing and turn over the top of the bag. If the bag is too full the icing will ooze out of the top. Remember always to squeeze from the top and never from the sides!

Icing for the decoration:
2 egg whites
450 g/1 lb/3½ cups icing sugar, sifted

Make up as before, taking note that the glycerine is not needed this time.

Pipe the scrolls round the base of each cake, a single row round the top edge of the small cake, and a double row round the top of the larger cake. Round the sides of the cakes we put flowers made with icing, piped on to squares of waxed paper, left overnight to harden, then taken off the paper and stored in an airtight tin until wanted. If you do not want to do this you could put a piece of ribbon round the sides.

To assemble the cakes on the day, put four cake pillars on the larger cake and put the top tier on them, and decorate as described on page 52.

* See page 53 for details of how to freeze the wedding cake.

Bouchées

Puff pastry:
225 g/8 oz/2 cups plain flour
pinch of salt
225 g/8 oz/1 cup butter
150 ml/¼ pint/generous ½ cup cold water

Sift the flour with the salt into a bowl and rub in a piece of the butter about the size of a walnut. Make a well in the centre and add the water. Mix it in using a round-bladed knife and then knead it for a minute or two only, to make a soft dough. Roll the pastry to a square about 1 cm/½ in thick. Beat the butter between two sheets of greaseproof paper to make it more pliable, place it in the centre of the pastry and wrap it up like a parcel. Wrap in a cloth or a piece of greaseproof paper and leave in a cool place for about 10 minutes. Put the dough on to a floured pastry board, flour the rolling pin, and press it down on the dough three or four times to flatten it slightly, then roll it out to a rectangle, about 1 cm/½ in thick, keeping the ends square. Fold the bottom third upwards, and the top third downwards, sealing the edges lightly with the rolling pin. Turn round so the edges are on the right like a book. This process is called a 'turn'. Repeat once more, then wrap it in the cloth or greaseproof paper and put in a cool place or the refrigerator to rest for 15 minutes. Do four more 'turns', putting the pastry to rest for 15 minutes after the fourth and the sixth turn. Leave in the refrigerator until wanted.

To make the bouchées:
Set the oven to 220°C/425°F/Gas Mark 7.

Roll the pastry out to about 1 cm/½ in thick, and using a 5 cm/2 in diameter fluted cutter cut out rounds. Place on a damp baking sheet, and brush with egg-wash, which is an egg beaten up with a ½ teaspoonful of salt. Using a smaller plain cutter 2.5 cm/1 in in diameter, cut only half-way through the bouchées, then put into the oven and bake for about 15 minutes, until well risen and golden brown. Take out and with a sharp pointed knife cut round the centre lid, scoop out a little of the dough inside and leave to cool. This recipe makes about 25 bouchées.

* These bouchée cases will keep well in an airtight tin for a week or two, or can be frozen for up to six months.

Fillings—the basic sauce:
900 ml/1½ pints/1 US quart milk
1 bay leaf
blade mace
sprig of thyme and parsley
50 g/2 oz/¼ cup margarine
50 g/2 oz/½ cup plain flour

Put the milk into a saucepan with the herbs, bring slowly to the boil, then strain. In a clean saucepan melt the margarine, add the flour, stir until smooth then pour on the flavoured milk. Stir until smooth then bring to the boil, stirring all the time, and boil for a minute or two. Divide into three and flavour each with the following fillings.

Chicken—add 200 g/7 oz/1½ cups finely chopped cooked chicken and seasoning to taste.

Mushroom—finely chop 100 g/4 oz/1⅓ cups mushrooms in a little butter, and add seasoning.

Shrimp—a small tin of shrimps and a few drops of Tabasco.

Fill the bouchée cases with the fillings, put on the lids and put into the oven for a few minutes to warm through, or they can be served cold.

Alabama Sauce and Fried Scampi

1 pepper
2–3 sticks of celery
1 clove garlic, crushed with a little salt
150 ml/¼ pint/generous ½ cup boiled dressing (see page 89)
1 teaspoon grated horseradish
2 tablespoons tomato chutney
a little sugar
salt and pepper
few drops of Tabasco sauce

450 g/1 lb scampi

Cut the pepper in half, remove the seeds and chop it fairly finely. Blanch it by putting it into cold water, bring it to the boil, then drain it and rinse under cold water, drain well. Chop the celery finely and add it to the dressing with the pepper, garlic, horseradish and tomato chutney. Season well with sugar, salt and pepper and Tabasco.

Egg and crumb the scampi and fry in deep fat, drain well on kitchen paper. Pour the sauce into a bowl and surround with the fried scampi. Stick a few cocktail sticks into some of the scampi for easier dipping.

Sandwiches

Asparagus rolls
Cut the crusts off a small brown loaf, butter it and cut into thin slices. Roll each slice of bread round a cooked head of asparagus, either fresh or tinned.

Other sandwich fillings can be tongue and mustard, finely sliced cucumber sprinkled with chopped mint, or chopped hard-boiled egg mixed with finely chopped watercress. Use a mixture of white and brown bread. Cut into triangles, remove the crusts and arrange on a serving dish.

* The asparagus rolls and sandwiches (except the egg and watercress) can all be frozen.

Coffee Meringues

225 g/8 oz/1 cup caster sugar
4 egg whites
1½ teaspoons/2 US teaspoons instant coffee powder

First of all grease two or three baking sheets with oil, sprinkle with a little flour and set aside while you make the meringues. If you are lucky enough to own a copper bowl, this is perfect for making meringues. For some strange reason the whites can be beaten stiffer more easily and one seems to get more bulk.

Put the egg whites into a clean bowl. (If using a copper bowl, clean it first with a little lemon juice or vinegar and salt, then rinse it with hot water and dry well.) Using a balloon whisk, whisk the whites until really stiff—this is very important. To tell if they are stiff enough, hold some of the whites on the whisk, and if they stand up in really firm peaks, they are stiff enough. When they are stiff, beat in 1 teaspoonful of the sugar for each egg white and continue to whisk for a few seconds only. Using a metal spoon, gently fold in the rest of the sugar and the coffee powder, being careful not to overdo the mixing as this is one of the causes of weeping meringues.

Fill a piping bag with a small vegetable rose pipe, and pipe the meringues on to the prepared baking sheets. Dust with a little caster sugar, and put into a slow oven, 110°C/225°F/Gas Mark ¼ and cook for about 1½ to 2 hours.

Leave to cool on a wire rack and when cool sandwich with 300 ml/½ pint/1¼ cups double cream, whipped and flavoured with a little coffee essence.

The meringue shells will keep for about a week in an airtight tin. The flavouring is inclined to make them go soft more quickly than usual.

Autumn Dinner Party (illustration page 63)

What could be more cheering than a mixture of reds for a table arrangement at an autumn dinner party. Vibrant, glowing colours to set the room alight on a misty, autumn evening. I love gathering scarlet berries and fruits whose glossy skins pick up all the highlights of fire and candles.

Here, the container is a black shallow iron vase which seems highly suitable for this type of arrangement. I would always advise using a shallow container for table flowers as it makes for a much easier arrangement than a high-sided vase where it is difficult to place the stems so that the blooms hang gracefully over the side. It helps if you sit down at the table and look at the vase before you start, because you see it from quite a different angle. If the vase or bowl is very deep you see a lot of it, so the shallower the vase the less you have to conceal. On the other hand, a vase raised on a stem adds elegance and seems to require fewer flowers to get the same effect, but be careful that the stem is not too tall or one has the old problem with table flowers—you cannot sit and talk comfortably through a bunch of flowers at eye-level. Dodging the flowers in order to carry on a conversation across the table is a situation definitely to be avoided.

From midsummer through to autumn is the ideal time of year for reds as there are so many flowers available for cutting from the garden: the last of the roses, often at their best in the autumn, dahlias, gladioli, sedum and pieces of lovely coloured autumn foliage, azalea, peony and viburnum. Azalea and *Viburnum opulus sterile* are both excellent as they last a long time and their leaves stay on the branches really well. But I try not to cut too many sprays of autumn foliage as they don't last all that long in water and it seems such a waste. Be sure to cut with great care so that you do not spoil the shape of the bush or tree by removing a vital branch.

The blending of apricot and deep red is important, as flowers which are all the same tone of red can make a dull and uninteresting arrangement. Here, I placed the fruits and peppers right in the centre at the base of the vase, to get the correct balance and followed this through to the top with some heavily berried spikes of the seed heads of *Arum italicum pictum*. This is a plant I have mentioned many times but never cease to enjoy, starting to pick the leaves in November and going right on to May. In every month they increase in size and here I have used the wonderfully brilliant scarlet seed heads.

In recent years I have come to realize that table flowers can really be complementary to the china or glass on the table and do not necessarily have to tone with everything in the room. This is particularly true in the evening when the lights are usually focused on the table and the room may be in partial darkness, and one is not so conscious of the surrounding colours of either furnishings or pictures. So concentrate on the colour of the dinner service or glass. I picked up the colour here by incorporating the red glass plates.

Pinks and mauves are also autumnal colours and I tend to forget this. But at this time of year we have the vivid blue of *Gentian sino-ornata*, the mauve of aster and michaelmas daisy. We have pinks and mauves in heaths or *Erica*, the soft pink of *Nerine bowdenii*, an autumn bulb that should be grown by anyone who has the shelter of a south wall. And let us not forget the lovely autumn crocus, *Colchicum*, in white and lilac pink—so many of these soft blues and pinks are part of the autumn flower garden.

Blues are difficult to use at night as they tend to go black and if you are doing an arrangement which you look at from a distance, I would advise against blue. But for a small dinner party where everyone is fairly close to the flowers I think it would show up quite well, and these soft pinks, mauves and blues can be most attractive.

So you can plan the colour scheme of your flowers, once you have decided on the colour of the china and table linen you are going to use. Or, as in my own case, this is often decided for me by my flowers as I know I have a few roses of a certain colour or some tulips, or polyanthus, depending on the time of year and the table arrangement has to follow suit.

The food for the dinner party could have been a choice of many things. Game, of course, comes to mind and with grouse, partridge and pheasant in season it is hard to choose. But Diana and I resisted game because we feel that lamb is so good at this time of year, still young, but large enough to make the best crown of lamb. This is such a spectacular dish to serve and gives a feeling of party straight away. The caviar mould is also good-looking and if you are out to impress I don't know of two better dishes to achieve this! Follow this with bramble and apple mousse with its lovely colour. It is a great pleasure to have fruits and vegetables in season when at all possible, as with so much frozen and imported food available today, the fresh home-growns are often overlooked.

Egg and Caviar Mould

1 jar caviar or lump fish roe approximately 175 g/6 oz
600 ml/1 pint/2½ cups aspic jelly *or*
15 g/½ oz/1 packet gelatine added to 600 ml/1 pint/2½ cups stock made from a stock cube
4 hard-boiled eggs
75 g/3 oz/½ cup shrimps

Put the caviar into the bottom of a straight-sided dish which holds 1.2 litres/2 pints/5 cups and pour over just enough of the aspic jelly to cover and leave it in a cool place to set. Cut the eggs in half, and separate the yolks from the whites and chop both, keeping them separate. When the caviar layer has set, put on the chopped egg white, pour over a little of the aspic jelly to just cover the whites and leave to set. Repeat with the chopped egg yolks and finally with the shrimps. Leave the mould in a cool place to set. To turn out the mould, dip the bowl in a basin of hot water for a few seconds only to loosen the edges, then turn out on to a serving dish.

Stuffed Crown of Lamb

1 crown of lamb made from 2 best ends of neck, each having 7–8 chops

For the stuffing:
1 small onion
50 g/2 oz/4 tablespoons butter or margarine
100 g/4 oz/1 $\frac{1}{3}$ cups chopped mushrooms
100 g/4 oz/2 cups fresh breadcrumbs
salt and pepper
25 g/1 oz/$\frac{1}{6}$ cup (firmly pressed down) dried apricots, soaked overnight
1 dessertspoon chopped parsley
1 egg

First prepare the crown of lamb. (A good butcher will usually do this for you, if he is asked in advance.) Failing that, it is not too difficult to prepare one yourself. Ask your butcher to chine the best ends of neck for you. This means cutting out the backbone.

Trim the meat off the ends of the bones, exposing about 4 cm/1 $\frac{1}{2}$ in and scrape the bones clean. Cut off the chine bone and make a little cut between the bones to enable the crown to curve round. Thread a trussing needle with string, hold the two best ends of neck back to back, sew the two pieces together at each end. When both ends have been joined, mould it into a round. Leave on one side while the stuffing is made.

To make the stuffing, peel and chop the onion. Melt the butter in a pan, add the chopped onion and cook until soft. Chop the mushrooms and add to the pan and cook quickly for a minute or two. Put the breadcrumbs into a bowl and add the onion and mushrooms with the seasoning and the drained, chopped apricots, and the chopped parsley. Beat the egg and add enough to bind the stuffing.

Stuff the centre of the crown with this stuffing and put it into a roasting tin with a little hot dripping. Put into a preheated oven 190°C/375°F/Gas Mark 5 and roast for 20 minutes per 450 g/1 lb and 20 minutes over. Take out and place on a warmed meat dish. Make the gravy by pouring off most of the fat in the roasting tin, sprinkle in about a tablespoon of flour and stir into a roux. Heat and cook until brown then pour on about 300 ml/$\frac{1}{2}$ pint/1 $\frac{1}{4}$ cups stock, stir well, bring to the boil and season to taste.

To garnish the crown:
8 dried apricot halves
8 mushroom caps
butter

Soak the apricots in water overnight, then cook in the same liquid until they are just tender. Drain and keep warm. Wipe the mushrooms and cook them in a little butter for a few minutes. Place the apricot halves and the mushroom caps alternately on the bones of the crown.

Roast Potatoes

1 kg/2 lb potatoes
dripping or oil

Peel the potatoes and cut into half or quarters depending on their size. Put into a pan with cold water, bring to the boil and boil for 5 minutes only, drain well, return them to the pan, put on the lid and gently shake the pan for a few seconds until the potatoes are roughened. Melt the dripping or the oil in a roasting tin in the oven, when it is hot add the potatoes, baste well and put on top shelf in the oven, 190°C/375°F/Gas Mark 5 for an hour or until cooked and brown. Drain on a piece of kitchen paper and serve at once, otherwise they are inclined to go soft.

The reason for roughening the skins before roasting potatoes is that the outsides roast nice and crisp instead of possibly becoming tough.

Bramble and Apple Mousse

225 g/½ lb cooking apples
450 g/1 lb blackberries
2 tablespoons granulated sugar
2 tablespoons water
juice of half a lemon
4 teaspoons gelatine
3 eggs (size 2–3/large)
75 g/3 oz/⅓ cup caster sugar
150 ml/¼ pint/generous ½ cup double cream

For decoration:
150 ml/¼ pint/generous ½ cup double cream
few blackberries

Peel, core and slice the apples and put in a pan with the blackberries and granulated sugar. Cook until pulpy, about 20–30 minutes. Sieve and leave to cool.

Put the water and lemon juice into a small pan, sprinkle on the gelatine and leave to soak.

With the eggs and caster sugar in a bowl whisk, either using a rotary beater over a pan of hot water or use an electric mixer, until thick and mousse-like. (If using an electric mixer *don't* place the bowl over hot water.) The mixture is thick enough if, when you hold the whisk up, the mixture running off it holds its shape on the mixture in the bowl. Measure 175 ml/6 fl oz/¾ cup of the fruit purée and add to the mousse mixture, dissolve the gelatine over a gentle heat then add to the mousse. Lightly whip the cream and fold in. Pour into a glass bowl and leave in a cool place to set.

To decorate, whip the cream until it will just hold its shape, and put into a piping bag fitted with a small vegetable rose pipe. Pour the remaining apple and blackberry purée on to the mousse, then pipe a lattice pattern over the top. Put blackberries where the lines of the lattice cross.

Cocktail Party (illustration page 66)

This is the simplest way to entertain a lot of people . . . one cocktail party and it takes care of a great many to whom you are indebted in one way or another. It is not my own favourite form of entertaining because my ears cannot take a lot of noise and, try as you may, it is almost impossible to keep the sound level down! On the other hand it is nice to meet all those people that one would rarely see but for an occasion like this.

Because of the number of people and the fact that they are generally standing, flowers should be really high up. If you have a plinth or a high shelf, there is no problem. But if not, a book case or bookshelves are a great help. Clear one shelf of books for the occasion and the space will make a striking setting for a long low arrangement of flowers. For this you need a very shallow container so that sprays of ivy or other drooping foliage may hang gracefully over the side of the container.

If you have no suitable place then I suggest you use the flowers as I have done, in a hanging arrangement. It is not always possible to drive in a nail to hang a metal basket but there are other ways. Perhaps you could remove a picture for the evening and use the nail for attaching the string of either a basket or simply a moist block of Oasis covered in kitchen foil and with a layer of wire mesh to hold the stems firmly. This can be hung either with ribbon or, if you use concealed string, I suggest that you finish off with a ribbon bow. Balls of flowers made in this way are very pretty. *Alchemilla mollis* makes a lime green, delicate fluffy ball which is decorative and lasts very well, and small balls of fruit blossom—apple or pear—are ideal if you have old trees that can stand this sort of pruning. Use garden roses in summer and for Christmas, balls of holly or mistletoe. All need ribbons hanging from the base, preferably in colours blending with the flowers.

As guests arrive a really striking arrangement gives a welcome. This can be put in the hall or in any room or passage on the way to the main room. If you have a narrow hall, then it is a good idea to have a hanging arrangement. A shallow round basket rather like a plate, hung with its under-side to the wall, facing outwards. At the base of the basket attach a small block of Oasis and cover with foil and wire mesh. To hold it in place thread a florist's wire through the length and breadth like tying up a parcel. The Oasis must be wet, but puncture the foil in several places and allow the Oasis to drain. Then put in the flower stems, making a small arrangement at the base of the basket. Again make a bow and long streamer ends so that they hang down below the finished arrangement.

Colour plays a very important part in decoration and it is best, for a party, to have something eye-catching, really gay and striking. And for this, reds are undoubtedly very successful. Brilliant reds always attract attention, and it is important that flowers for special occasions should stand out and make their presence felt.

In this arrangement the red rose in the middle is 'Fragrant Cloud' and just behind it is the two-tone 'Typhoo Tea', while the deep red rose in the front is 'Ena Harkness', which is still for me one of the most lovely and fragrant roses. Hanging over the edge is 'Rosemary Rose', whose nice, flat open face makes it ideal for the flower arranger. Its arching sprays too, help to give those flowing lines so necessary for a hanging or raised vase.

Melini

As in all mixed-red flower arrangements the touch of orange is essential as it suddenly makes the whole vase come to life. Here I have used the stems of *Alstroemeria ligtu* hybrids, these useful perennials that make a lovely show in the garden and last extremely well as a cut flower. The other touch of apricot is one of the fluffy peony-flowered poppies. Lastly, a mauvy, cerise sweet pea called 'The Doctor', a fairly new sweet pea from Unwins. The blended colours of red are always stimulating.

Talking of red roses it is interesting to remember that when we were doing the flowers for the Coronation we were sent a marvellous collection of red roses, gladioli, and carnations from the European flower growers. But when arranged they were so much on the same colour plane that they became dull and uninteresting. So Mrs Spry got permission to 'cut' in Kew Gardens and came back with armfuls of apricot azaleas and some mauve rhododendrons and it was these sprays mixed in the arrangements which brought them suddenly to life. It was such a striking change that it is a lesson I will never forget. So when making an arrangement of this kind, remember to have as many different shades and tones as possible.

I strongly advise against putting flowers on the bar or the buffet as these tend to get in the way when there are a lot of people about and food is being served. Should you be having a buffet with service, which I should imagine is highly unlikely in these days, then I suggest a large tazza-type vase filled with decorative fruit and some bold leaves of vine, or bay, or variegated ivy in winter.

Food for the cocktail party is much the same as for the wedding, but I do think that hot savouries, small quiches—really just mouthful size—hot sausages, water chestnuts wrapped in bacon, small cheese aigrettes are all welcome additions to all the good things which Diana has suggested.

Another delicious titbit is fresh almonds peeled and tossed in butter until they are just turning colour, then rolled in salt. They are irresistible.

When planning a cocktail party remember to keep the food bite-size. As we were only given one pair of hands we find it difficult to hold any more than a bite-size morsel. Apart from the guests' convenience the hostess will not really want too many crumbs on her carpets.

Sausage Rolls

300 g/10 oz/2½ cups plain flour
pinch of salt
225 g/8 oz/1 cup margarine, straight from the refrigerator
water to mix
450 g/1 lb sausage meat
beaten egg

Sift the flour into a bowl and add the salt. Using a coarse grater, grate the margarine into the flour, stir well with a round-bladed knife, then add enough water to make a dough. Be careful not to make it too soft. Put it in a cool place to rest for about ½ hour, wrapped in a piece of greaseproof paper.

Roll the sausage meat into 3 or 4 long rolls. Roll out the pastry, fairly thinly, and cut the edges straight. Lay a roll of sausage meat on the pastry, damp the edge of the pastry, and fold over the sausage meat, press the edges of pastry together to seal them. Continue in this way until all the sausage meat has been used. Cut the long rolls into 4–5 cm/1½–2 in lengths, brush with the beaten egg, put on to a baking tray and bake 200°C/400°F/Gas Mark 6 for 15–20 minutes. Cool on a wire tray. The quantities should make about 45 sausage rolls.

* Sausage rolls can be stored in the freezer for about one month.

Cheese Sables

75 g/3 oz/¾ cup plain flour
pinch cayenne pepper
75 g/3 oz/⅓ cup butter
75 g/3 oz/⅔ cup grated cheese
beaten egg
25 g/1 oz/¼ cup chopped mixed nuts

Sift the flour and cayenne pepper into a bowl, rub in the butter, add the cheese, and mix to a dough. Roll out to a square, brush with the beaten egg and sprinkle on the chopped nuts, lightly pressing them in. Cut into squares, then into triangles, place on a piece of greaseproof paper in a baking tray. (The reason for the greaseproof paper is that once they are cooked they must be taken off the tray quickly so they do not overcook.) Bake in a preheated oven 200°C/400°F/Gas Mark 6 for 10–15 minutes.

Cheese Straws

100 g/4 oz/1 cup plain flour
50 g/2 oz/¼ cup butter
50 g/2 oz/½ cup grated cheese
1 tablespoon water
1 egg yolk

Sift the flour into a bowl and rub in the butter, stir in the cheese, mix the water with the yolk and add to the rubbed-in mixture to make a dough. Roll out, cut into strips and lay on a baking tray and bake in a preheated oven 200°C/400°F/Gas Mark 6 for 12–15 minutes. Cool on a wire tray.

Bouchées

The pastry and baking are the same as for the wedding reception (page 57), but make the bouchées slightly smaller.

Fillings—the basic sauce:
300 ml/½ pint/1¼ cups milk
4 peppercorns
bay leaf
sprig of parsley
25 g/1 oz/2 tablespoons butter
25 g/1 oz/3 tablespoons flour

Put the milk into a pan with the peppercorns, bay leaf and parsley, bring slowly to boiling point then strain. In a clean pan melt the butter, add the flour and stir it to make a roux, pour on the flavoured milk then bring to the boil, stirring all the time, adjust the seasoning. Pour into a basin, cover with a piece of damp greaseproof paper and leave to cool.

Curried egg filling:
2 hard-boiled eggs
1 teaspoon curry paste

Chop the hard-boiled eggs fairly finely, add the curry paste. Mix this into half the basic white sauce, and using a teaspoon, fill the bouchées.

Ham filling:
100 g/4 oz/½ cup ham

Finely chop or mince the ham and add to the remaining half of the white sauce. Then spoon into the bouchée cases as before.

If you want to serve these warm, heat them through in the oven for a few minutes.

Dips

Below are two dips, avocado to serve with the cheese straws, potato crisps and plain salted biscuits, and a mayonnaise flavoured with Tabasco and tomato in which to dip fried breaded scampi.

Avocado dip:
2 large ripe avocado pears
lemon juice
150 ml/¼ pint/generous ½ cup soured cream or plain yoghurt

Cut the avocados in half, remove the stones, and scoop out the flesh into a bowl and lightly mash it, adding a squeeze of lemon juice. Stir in the soured cream and serve fairly soon after mixing as the avocado is likely to turn black and will not look so appealing.

Mayonnaise dip:
300 ml/½ pint/1¼ cups mayonnaise
Tabasco sauce
tomato purée
pinch cayenne pepper

Mix all the seasonings into the mayonnaise, stirring in well to suit your taste.

Smoked Salmon Cartwheels

white bread
brown bread
butter
lemon juice
thin slices of smoked salmon

If you are fortunate you may be able to get an end of a side of smoked salmon which is cheaper than buying the slices.

Cut the crust off the bottom of the loaves and cut thin slices along the length of the bottom. Spread with butter, cut off the crusts, and lay on the slices of smoked salmon, sprinkle over a little lemon juice and freshly ground black pepper. Roll up as for a swiss roll,* then cut into short slices.

* Freeze at this stage.

Hallowe'en Party

This is a time for children, and a party that is celebrated more in America than in England, though I think that it is becoming more popular—and so it should as it is great fun. It is essentially a festival of the Irish and the Scots, was celebrated in Druid times and was sometimes called the Festival of the Dead, hence the association with ghosts, witches and graveyards. It was celebrated on the first of November and its eve on the thirty-first of October was known in the Old Celtic calendar as 'the old year's night'. In Christian times the festival became dedicated to the saints and All Saints Day is celebrated on the first of November.

Party time means dressing up as witches and ghosts and bobbing for apples—you fill a bucket three-quarters full of water and place in it several apples and the game is to try to get your head into the bucket and pick one out with your teeth!

The colours for Hallowe'en are orange and black, so you can use black crêpe paper on the table and the orange gives one lots of scope for decorating with fruits and flowers.

This informal party is planned for twelve people of all ages, and we have chosen food which can all be eaten with either fingers or a fork, apart from the soup! First a really rich vegetable soup, excellent for a cold night, and then a quiche which is a little different and very popular with the young. The chicken drumsticks, with an excellent barbecue sauce, are delicious, as are baked potatoes served the American way with soured cream and bacon crisps. Lastly, the pumpkin tartlets were made from the inside of the pumpkin which we hollowed out for the decoration! They do need quite a lot of cinnamon, I think, or they tend to be a little tasteless.

Before I hollowed out the pumpkin I made a circle and cut off the top as a lid—this is important as the lid has to be left off when you light the night light. Before scooping out the inside, mark the details of the face on the pumpkin—two eyes, a triangle for the nose, and a slit mouth with chunky teeth! Then remove the inside keeping the flesh carefully for the filling for the pumpkin tartlets. You can freeze this if you don't want to use it at once. The night light gives a very effective touch but be sure to leave off the lid while it is alight. You can, of course, cunningly place an electric bulb in the centre if you like. I found the pumpkin lasted very well indeed, at least two weeks, and was most popular.

The fruit cone was made from a cone of small mesh wire netting. I found it best to roll this into shape, like making an icing bag cone, and then cut the wire straight at the bottom. Fill with crushed-up damp Oasis, (I save all my old pieces of Oasis in a plastic bag every time I clear a vase) and then place it on an urn type of vase. Working round the base you will keep it balanced, though you can secure it with a little piece of plasticine if you feel happier. The fruits were a mixture of tomatoes for their lovely colour, grapes, nuts, crab- or small apples, damsons and dark plums giving the dark, and black effect to enhance the black and orange theme. I wired the grapes, but just spiked the other fruits with cocktail sticks. A base of variegated leaves gives the finishing touch and one or two heads of open roses, of either 'Apricot Nectar' or 'Whisky Mac'. But you could use pompon dahlias and get a good effect if roses are hard to come by.

A short cut, instead of using wire for the cone, is to buy one of the readily available polystyrene cones. Any of the firm-stemmed flowers will press easily into these cones, and the method of the cocktail stick for the fresh fruit is, of course, the same. As these cones are also very light and a little difficult to balance I suggest that you start putting things in all round the base and then gradually work up to the top. Should you intend the cone to stand on a buffet table, as I feel in this case it would, then you need not be quite so particular about the back of the cone, but it needs covering with something like small sprigs of box and one or two larger fruits to keep it balanced.

Pumpkins are plentiful in Britain now, not quite to the extent that they are in the States where every roadside stall is a wonderful sight with pumpkins and gourds piled high, hanging with bunches of decorative sweetcorn, and selling casks and bottles of delicious fresh apple cider—a spectacle I will never forget. The Americans also hang a decoration on their doors at this time of year, especially if they are having a party. Often simply a bunch of sweetcorn grasses or some dried seed heads, tied with ribbons, and sometimes I have seen a huge basket of gourds or pumpkins on the doorstep, and such a lovely welcome it gives.

Hallowe'en Soup

750 g/1½ lb mixed root vegetables, diced small
handful small pasta shells
1.7 litres/3 pints/7 cups stock

To enhance the flavour always lightly brown the vegetables in a deep, heavy pan using 50–75 g/2–3 oz/¼ cup butter. Then pour in the hot stock, season with salt and pepper, and cook until tender. Then add the pasta shells, and if liked some tomatoes, either fresh (skinned, de-seeded and roughly chopped) or canned tomatoes. Simmer the soup until cooked.

Pour into a soup tureen for serving and sprinkle with some chopped parsley.

Sausage Quiche

For the pastry:
225 g/8 oz/2 cups plain flour
pinch of salt
50 g/2 oz/¼ cup butter or margarine
50 g/2 oz/¼ cup lard
2 tablespoons water

For the filling:
750 g/1½ lb chipolata sausages
1 medium onion
40 g/1½ oz/1½ tablespoons butter
4 eggs
450 ml/16 fl oz/1 US pint milk
pinch of mixed herbs
salt and black pepper
5 drops Worcestershire sauce

First of all make the pastry. Sift the flour into a basin with the salt and rub the fat into the flour until it resembles fine breadcrumbs. Add enough water to make a firm dough. Place in refrigerator for 20 minutes. Roll the pastry out and use to line a flan ring 28 cm/11 in. Leave in a cool place while the filling is prepared.

To make the filling, drop a little fat into a roasting tin, put in the sausages and place in a preheated oven, 190°C/375°F/Gas Mark 5 to part-cook them, for 20 minutes. Slice the onion. Melt the butter in a pan, add the onion slices and cook slowly until they just begin to turn brown. Break the eggs into a bowl, add the milk and the herbs, salt, pepper and Worcestershire sauce, then add the cooked onions. Take the sausages from the oven and arrange them in the pastry case to resemble the spokes of a wheel, then pour in the egg mixture. Put the flan into the oven, 190°C/375°F/Gas Mark 5 for 40–45 minutes, or until the filling is firm and golden brown. This can be served either hot or cold.

Chicken Drumsticks with Barbecue Sauce

Barbecue sauce:
50 g/2 oz/¼ cup butter
100 g/4 oz/⅔ cup onion, chopped
1 kg/2 lb tomatoes, fresh or tinned
4 sticks celery, chopped
5 tablespoons vinegar
2 tablespoons tomato ketchup
1 tablespoon Worcestershire sauce
2½ tablespoons demerara sugar
2 bay leaves
bouquet garni

12 chicken drumsticks
melted butter or oil

First, make the sauce. Melt the butter in a saucepan and put in the chopped onion and cook slowly until it is soft but not brown. Then add all the other ingredients, bring them to the boil and simmer for about 20 minutes. Pour through a strainer into a clean pan. If the sauce seems too thin, boil it to reduce a little.

To cook the drumsticks, brush them with the melted butter or oil and lay them in a roasting tin and put into a preheated oven, 200°C/400°F/Gas Mark 6 for about 30 minutes, turning them over once. To prevent the guests' fingers getting too greasy, put a cutlet frill on the end of each drumstick or wrap a piece of greaseproof paper round the end. Arrange them on a dish and serve with the sauce.

Baked Potatoes with Soured Cream and Bacon Crisps

Choose potatoes roughly the same size and scrub them well. Rub all over with salt and prick several times with a fork. This helps to prevent them bursting while they are in the oven. Put the potatoes into a preheated oven 180°C/350°F/Gas Mark 4 for 1–1½ hours. The cooking time will depend on the size of the potatoes. When they are cooked, take them out of the oven, cut the potatoes open by cutting a cross on top and open by pushing up from the bottom.

100 g/4 oz streaky bacon
142 ml/5 fl oz soured cream

Cut the bacon into small pieces and fry quickly until crisp, drain on kitchen paper and leave to cool. Pour the soured cream into a serving bowl and sprinkle the bacon crisps on top. Arrange the cooked potatoes round the sauce.

Pumpkin Tartlets

For the pastry:
225 g/8 oz/2 cups plain flour
pinch of salt
150 g/5 oz/¾ cup lard or shortening
2–3 tablespoons cold water.

For the filling:
450 g/1 lb raw pumpkin
2 eggs
300 ml/½ pint/ 1¼ cups evaporated milk
100 g/4 oz/¾ cup soft brown sugar
1 teaspoon ground cinnamon
½ teaspoon ground ginger
¼ teaspoon ground nutmeg

First make the pastry. Sift the flour with the salt into a mixing bowl and rub in the shortening. Add enough water to make a firm dough, and leave in a cool place for 30 minutes. Roll the dough out fairly thinly and line about 24 tartlet tins.

Cut up the pumpkin flesh and put into a pan with a little water and cook until tender. This will take about 15–20 minutes. Drain well and mash.

Break the eggs into a bowl and beat well, add the evaporated milk, the pumpkin purée, sugar and spices and mix well together. Spoon this mixture into the tartlet cases and put into a preheated oven 190°C/375°F/Gas Mark 5 for 20–30 minutes. As the pastry is very short it is best to leave the tarts to get cold before removing from the tins.

Thanksgiving Party (illustration page 75)

The fourth Thursday in November is the big day in America. The day on which all Americans give thanks for safe landings in their beloved land, and, in celebration of the settlers' first harvest, the traditional foods eaten are those that were available to the first Americans—the wild turkey, cranberries, pumpkins and blueberries. Thanksgiving has become a real family occasion and is celebrated now as a family gathering more than Christmas. Christmas may be spent often in a warm climate or skiing, but all families work towards having a get-together for Thanksgiving.

Decorating starts with a welcome on the door. Nearly everyone makes a wreath for the door and unlike the Christmas wreath they are made mostly of dried materials. Often the base of the wreath is straw and these are sold in florists' shops. They are about 20 cm/8 in in diameter with firmly packed straw on a frame and they can be decorated with a spray of dried flowers—like *Helichrysum* (straw flowers) and grasses and seed heads of different kinds, with decorative corn cobs tied at the base. Last year I saw a very pretty wreath made out of dried sea lavender, with the traditional spray at the base made with gourds, drieds and corn. Straw wreaths which are bound with olive green ribbon need only a very small spray of drieds to finish them off.

Often, instead of a wreath, just a bunch of decorative corn tied with a ribbon bow is hung on the door, or a spray with gourds and corn. I found while I was in America that I used Oasis Sec, a dry, hard Oasis which stays firm when you want to place in it dry or semi-dried flowers and seed heads. You can cut it into a shape, oval or round, or just use it in its oblong shape which makes a good spray and is effective decorated with preserved eucalyptus, preserved beech leaves, pine cones, straw flowers, achillea heads, grasses and dry bits of hydrangea.

Sometimes if the door was very beautiful or had no place for hanging a decoration, then you would find a prettily arranged trug basket with gourds and corn, perhaps brightly coloured peppers, and sprays of the lovely magnolia leaves either dark green while still fresh, or brown after treatment in glycerine and water (one part glycerine and two water). You can see a green one at the top of the dried arrangement in the photograph.

The candle is in a wooden hanging container which I bought in Kentucky at the restored Shaker Town Center in Louisville, where it is possible to buy some of the copies of the original candle sconces, jugs and bowls. I brought the glass home carried over my arm. As you can see it arrived perfectly safely. You can also use it without the glass, placing a small bowl where the candle normally stands and arranging the flowers as a hanging container. Here I placed the glass and candle well back and put a small group of flowers in a container at the side. This mixture of dried and fresh is an ideal type of arrangement for winter whether you are having a party or not, and really gives the best effect I know for this time of year. You can ring the changes by changing the fresh flowers for some apricot roses, or hydrangea flower heads or by removing altogether and adding more dried pieces, like achillea or some bought drieds—lotus heads or wood roses—something rather special.

The hanging basket idea is good for a small hall if you are having a cocktail party, or any party with a lot of people in a small space. Take the round shallow basket and dry polystyrene or Oasis Sec—as these are all dried it is not necessary to use wet Oasis—then cut a piece about 75 mm/3 in square and tie it on to the basket with thin florist's wire that will go round the hard block, round the length and breadth, as in a paper parcel, and twist the wire at the back until it is quite secure. Then place into it some dried things. Here I have some hanging stems of bittersweet, native of North America, growing over hedges and ditches in many areas. The pods of the lovely milkweed are full of fluffy cotton-like seeds when you pick them in the autumn which, sadly but necessarily, have all to be carefully removed or they fly about everywhere and are really a problem. I have tried spraying them with lacquer but it is not one hundred per cent successful. An interesting thing about this plant is that it is where the Monarch moth lays its eggs. These pods dry well and stay a good natural green. The achillea is best dried in a pot with a little water. I find that if you tie them in bunches and hang them upside down in the ordinary way, the stems tend to press into the heads and spoil the perfect shape. You can powder the heads with borax for better colour, though I am never sure if it is really worth the extra trouble. Pine cones and large glycerined magnolia leaves complete the arrangement.

The little corn dolly that is hanging from the base of the basket is traditionally British. They were made in the days long ago to decorate the corn stacks—which goes to show how much more time there was then to make beautiful things like this. They were often made with the ears of corn tucked away inside and these were then removed in spring, beautifully dry and ready to plant. However, the art is still practised on farms and many members of the Women's Institute go in for this traditional craft. It is a delight to see these enchanting little straw designs still made in this technological age.

The turkey is traditionally the main course for the celebration of Thanksgiving and, naturally, we have chosen to have one. To start the meal we have an interesting avocado salad and the sweet is a pie made with American pastry but, of course, you could always use an ordinary shortcrust or French Pâte Sucrée. As usual we have catered for 6.

Avocado Starter

3 oranges
3 grapefruit
3 ripe avocado pears
french dressing
chopped parsley

First of all prepare the citrus fruit. Using a knife with a serrated edge, cut off the tops and then cut round the fruit in a spiral fashion removing the peel and the pith. Divide the fruit into segments and put into a bowl.

Cut the avocado pears in half and remove the stones. Peel off the skin and cut the flesh into fingers, lengthwise. Arrange round the outside of an avocado pear dish and place the oranges and grapefruit segments in the middle. Pour over a little french dressing (see overleaf), garnish with chopped parsley and serve.

As the avocado pears tend to discolour, it is not a good idea to prepare them much in advance. This does not apply, of course, to the citrus fruits.

French dressing:
crushed garlic to taste
pinch of sugar
salt and pepper
3 tablespoons oil
1 tablespoon wine or cider vinegar

Put the crushed garlic, sugar and seasoning into a bowl, add the oil and vinegar and whisk all well together.

Roast Turkey

For the stuffing:
50 g/2 oz/½ cup dried apricots
2 medium-sized onions
1 small head of celery
40 g/1½ oz/3 tablespoons butter
100 g/4 oz/1 cup chopped nuts, walnuts preferably or a mixture of nuts
50 g/2 oz/1 cup fresh white breadcrumbs
1 tablespoon chopped parsley
salt and freshly ground pepper

5–6 kg/12 lb turkey
butter

Soak the apricots in water overnight, drain them and cut them into small pieces. Peel the onions and chop them. Wash the celery and cut the sticks into thin slices.

Melt the butter in a large pan, add the onions and cook until they are soft but not brown. Add the sliced celery, apricots and the chopped nuts. Cook over a brisk heat for about 4 minutes, stirring all the time, then allow to cool. Stir in the breadcrumbs and the chopped parsley, and season to taste.

Put this stuffing in the neck end of the bird, under the skin, tuck the flap under and secure with a skewer, then mould the stuffed breast to a nice round end.

To roast the turkey:
Below are two ways of cooking the turkey—a slow method and a quicker one. For the slower method, rub the butter all over the bird and wrap it in greaseproof paper or foil, put into a roasting tin in a preheated oven 170°C/325°F/Gas Mark 3, cook for 20 minutes per 450 g/1 lb and 30 minutes over. To test if the bird is cooked, push a skewer into the thigh and drumstick. The juice that runs out should be quite clear. If it is still on the pink side, put the turkey back into the oven for a little longer. Cover with damp cloth while gravy is prepared.

The other method of cooking the turkey is to rub the butter all over it as before, cover with a piece of greaseproof paper, and put the bird in a roasting tin. Pour round about 600 ml/1 pint/2½ cups good turkey stock made from the giblets, and put into a preheated oven, 180°C/350°F/Gas Mark 4 and cook for 15 minutes per 450 g/1 lb and 15 minutes over, basting it several times during the cooking. Test as before to check if turkey is cooked and cover with a damp cloth while the gravy is made and the vegetables are dished up.

Creamed Sweetcorn

450 g/1 lb frozen sweetcorn or some sweetcorn kernels
salt and pepper
small carton double cream

Cook the sweetcorn in boiling salted water until they are tender. Drain well, season, and keep warm. Pour over the cream immediately before serving.

Creamed Potatoes

1.5 kg/3 lb potatoes
salt
25 g/1 oz/2 tablespoons butter
350 ml/12 fl oz/1½ cups milk

Peel potatoes and cook until soft, then mash well or put through a sieve or a potato-ricer. Add the butter and warmed milk and beat well.

Cranberry Sauce

450 g/1 lb cranberries
150 ml/¼ pint/generous ½ cup water
100 g/4 oz/½ cup granulated sugar
1 tablespoon port

Wash the cranberries and put them into a saucepan with the water and bring to the boil. Simmer until the berries are cooked and pulpy, adding a little extra water if necessary. Add the sugar and stir until it is all dissolved, then add the port.

* This sauce freezes very well.

Blueberry Pie

For the pastry:
225 g/8 oz/2 cups self-raising flour
pinch of salt
150 g/5 oz/¾ cup lard
2–3 tablespoons cold water

For the filling:
750 g/1½ lb/5 cups fresh blueberries
2 tablespoons plain flour
175 g/6 oz/¾ cup caster sugar

First, make the pastry. Sift the flour with the salt into a bowl and rub the fat into it, adding the water to make a dough. Leave in a cool place for 30 minutes. Divide the pastry in two and put one half aside for the top. Roll out one half and line a pie plate 20 cm/8 in in diameter.

Roll out the other half of the pastry, slightly larger than before and leave it while the filling is prepared.

Put the blueberries into a basin, add the flour and the sugar and mix all together, then put into the lined pie plate. Damp the edges and cover with the other piece of rolled out pastry, pressing well together. Mark the edges with a fork and prick the top pastry with the fork in a pattern.

Put into the preheated oven 200°C/400°F/Gas Mark 6 for 40–45 minutes. Take from the oven, sprinkle the top with caster sugar and serve either hot or cold.

* This pie can be frozen.

Winter's Day Luncheon Party (illustration page 78)

Our winter's day lunch is for those who are out hunting or shooting or beagling or fishing or maybe just walking, and even if you are not the energetic type it's still good on a cold day!

We have arranged a menu which, whatever time of day the party actually comes in, the food will still be excellent. An old-fashioned steak and kidney pudding is a marvellous standby at a time like this and, personally, I have never found a man in my life who has not loved it. Lining the crust with a few oysters makes it even more special. If you are really very uncertain about the time they will arrive, then I would cut out the leeks as they need to be freshly cooked, but the red cabbage (not shown in the photograph) is ideal.

The dried flower arrangement seemed suitable for this luncheon but I could not resist the touch of spring in the small arrangement at the side. Both were arranged in shallow copper platters, the dried in a well pin-holder and the fresh pieces in a small bowl filled with Oasis. The tiny pale blossoms are *Viburnum fragrans* which with its mass of pale pink flowers is a delight on a mild winter's day when the leafless dark stems are covered with these sweetly scented clusters. *V. bodnantense*, a winter-flowering hybrid has a similar form but very much deeper pink flowers and I would thoroughly recommend both. Then come the sprays of the yellow winter jasmine and what a joy this little climbing flower can be. It is very well known but I still think it could be grown more widely. *Calluna vulgaris* 'H. E. Beale' is for me one of the best of the heaths, densely covered as it is with tapering sprays of deep pink flowers. When out they can be dried off and still be pink and pretty at the end of the winter. I would always advise cutting the sprays in October (in Britain) and putting them in shallow water in a warm room as they dry a better colour like this.

You can often find a few late-flowerers, an odd rose blooming well into winter, polyanthus which blooms intermittently all winter, and a precious bluey-mauve pansy or viola called 'Molly Briton', and I have often had the luck to find enough for a bowl-full at Christmas. Here I covered the Oasis with moss, useful if you are making a larger arrangement as moss hides all the mechanics and gives added moisture to keep these very short-stemmed little flowers alive.

The dried arrangement is a mixture of different flowers which have come from various places. The green milkweed pod seed heads, which I talked about earlier on page 77, when I used them in the Thanksgiving arrangement, grow all over the northern part of America and I can't wait to pick them and use them when I visit in the autumn. Those and the sedum and the grasses are all dried by hanging them upside down and removing all the lovely seeds from the milkweed pods before they smother the whole room. At the back there is a stem of *Mahonia bealei*, burnished brown after being treated with a solution of glycerine and water. To get this effect you place the stems in one part of glycerine and two parts of water and patiently wait. These sturdy leaves take quite a long time to absorb the glycerine, as long as six weeks, but well worth waiting for. Other plants that are good subjects for glycerine but take even longer, are aspidistra, and the newly formed catkins of *Garrya elliptica*. Aspidistra takes about six months but do not despair—and the garrya about six weeks. It is quite easy to tell when the glycerine has gone to the top of the leaf as you can literally see the colour changing up the stem, from green to brown.

Molucella laevis is also treated in glycerine and hence the change in colour from bright green to this creamy yellow. Here, as soon as they were fully open, I placed them in the glycerine right to the top of the stems. If you do it too early you lose the topmost florets. Leave for about five days—if you leave them too long they tend to go very soft—and then take them out and hang them upside down which enables the glycerine to run down into the heads.

The flowers right in the centre are a form of *Ipomoea*, one of the wood rose family which come from Hawaii with a round brown centre surrounded by cream petal-like bracts. I bought these but never have seen them growing. The lotus seed heads which I always thought were tropical came, in fact, from Indianapolis. On the right *Eryngium giganteum*, a thistley-type plant which once you have established it will be with you forever. It seeds freely and is marvellous as a dried seed head and equally useful as a fresh flower in the centre of any green group in summer.

The piece of dried fungus is more than useful. I like to dry any I can find and let me give you a tip—dry it very slowly. I heated mine too quickly and found that it curled up and soon shrivelled; on top of a warm radiator is ideal, or even in the linen cupboard, but I did find they smelt a bit.

All dried materials are much more interesting when used with a few fresh flowers. But if you make a permanent dried group then it is always possible to add a few fresh flowers as and when you have a special occasion. You can do this by putting the fresh flowers into a little Oasis, covering it with some foil or plastic and then tucking them into the vase of dried.

Another idea for a winter party would be to make a pot-et-fleur by using a mixture of potted plants and putting a container of water into the planted dish to which you might add some fresh cut flowers from time to time. A large tureen or copper bowl or even a wash-hand basin of bygone days, all make ideal containers for holding a mixture of plants and cut flowers—mixed ferns, begonias, peperomia, etc. In fact, any nice foliage plants. Keep them in their pots and arrange them with the taller subjects at the back of the bowl.

Artichoke Soup

3 medium onions
75 g/3 oz/$\frac{1}{3}$ cup butter
1 kg/2 lb artichokes (Jerusalem)
600 ml/1 pint/$2\frac{1}{2}$ cups water
2 tablespoons flour
600 ml/1 pint/$2\frac{1}{2}$ cups hot milk
salt and pepper

Peel and finely slice the onions. Melt the butter in a pan, add the onions and soften without colouring, add the peeled and sliced artichokes and cook for a few minutes. Pour on the water, bring to the boil and allow to simmer for 20–30 minutes or until the artichokes are cooked. Put through a sieve or liquidize.* Return to a clean pan. Blend the flour with a little extra milk and add to the soup with the hot milk and the salt and pepper. Stir until it comes to the boil then cook for a few minutes before serving.

* The soup can be frozen at this stage in the recipe.

Beefsteak and Kidney Pudding

For the filling:
1 kg/2 lb skirt or stewing steak
1 small onion
175 g/6 oz ox kidney
1 tablespoon plain flour
salt and pepper

For the suet pastry:
225 g/8 oz/2 cups self-raising flour
salt
100 g/4 oz/1 cup shredded suet
cold water

A pudding basin, with a 15 cm/6 in diameter top and holding 900 ml/1½ pints/1 US quart will be needed.

Cut the beef into 2 cm/¾ in cubes approximately. Chop the onion and add to the beef. Cut the ox kidney into cubes also. Add the flour with some salt and pepper and mix all together so that the meat is well coated.

Now make the pastry. Sift the flour with the salt into a bowl. If using fresh suet, remove the skin and either chop finely or grate it (I find this method easier) and add to the flour. Add enough cold water to make a not too sticky dough and knead it until it is smooth. Grease the basin well with a little melted fat. Take about two-thirds of the pastry and roll into a circle about 2 cm/¾ in thick. To line the basin with this, dust the pastry well with flour and fold it in half, then press the side edges together, and gently roll the folded end to elongate it. The pastry should now look like a bag. Gently put your hand between the two layers, support pastry with other hand and lift it into the greased basin. Work the pastry so that it lines the basin evenly and about 2 cm/¾ in of pastry stands up above the top of the basin. Fill the lined basin with the meat and pour in enough cold water to come just over half-way to the top. Roll out the remaining third of the pastry to fit the top. Damp the edges and put on the lid, sealing the edges well. Cover with a double piece of greaseproof paper, well greased and with a large pleat in the centre to allow the pudding to rise. Cover this loosely with kitchen foil and tie on with a piece of string. To make it easier to lift in and out of the pan, tie a loop of string over the top to form a handle. Have ready a pan of boiling water, and put in the pudding, cover with the lid and boil for 3 to 4 hours. Do not let the pan run dry during boiling and always top up with boiling water. When cooked, take out of the pan, remove the paper and foil coverings. Cut out a piece of pastry and pour in some extra boiling water into the filling to give it a little extra juice. To serve, wrap a clean napkin round the basin.

Ragout of Veal

1 kg/2 lb stewing veal
1 medium onion
225 g/½ lb tomatoes
100 g/4 oz mushrooms
3 tablespoons oil
1 tablespoon plain flour
400 ml/¾ pint/1¾ cups chicken stock
150 ml/¼ pint/generous ½ cup white wine
salt and pepper

Cut the veal into 2.5 cm/1 in cubes. Slice the onion. Skin the tomatoes by pouring boiling water over them, count to twenty, pour off the water and then pour over cold water. The skins should now come off very easily. Cut into quarters and remove the seeds. Wash the mushrooms, and, if large, cut into quarters otherwise leave whole.

Heat the oil, add the veal and brown on both sides. Take out and keep warm, put the sliced onion in the pan and soften. Add the flour and cook for a few minutes until it is straw coloured, pour in the stock and the wine and add the veal. Bring to the boil and add the mushrooms and season. Put into the oven 180°C/350°F/Gas Mark 4 for 1–1½ hours. Halfway through the cooking add the tomatoes.

Serve with creamed potatoes.

To serve with both the ragout and the pudding, here is a selection of vegetables.

Braised Onions

6 large onions
butter
salt and pepper
sugar

Peel the onions and put into a pan of cold water, bring to the boil and cook for a few minutes only. This process makes them more digestible. Butter an ovenproof dish and put in the onions, sprinkle with salt and pepper and brush them with a little melted butter. Sprinkle over a little sugar and bake in the oven at 190°C/375°F/Gas Mark 5 until tender, about 1–1½ hours.

Glazed Carrots

700 g/1½ lb carrots
½ teaspoon salt
25 g/1 oz/2 tablespoons butter
1 teaspoon sugar

Peel the carrots and, depending on their size, either leave them whole or cut them into quarters lengthwise. Put into a pan with cold water to just cover. Add the salt, butter and sugar, cover with the lid and bring to the boil. Boil until they are just tender (about 15 minutes), then remove the lid and boil faster until almost all the liquid has evaporated. Take off the heat before the liquid completely evaporates, as the sugar will caramelize very easily and the end result will not be very appetizing! Also be careful not to add too much salt. Serve at once.

Leeks in a White Sauce

1 kg/2 lb leeks

For the white sauce:
20 g/¾ oz/1½ tablespoons butter
20 g/¾ oz/2 tablespoons plain flour
300 ml/½ pint/1¼ cups milk
salt and pepper

Trim off some of the green tops of the leeks, cut off the roots, and wash the leeks well. If very muddy, you may have to cut them lengthwise to clean them, but they look much nicer if kept whole. Place the leeks in a pan of boiling, salted water and cook until tender, about 20 minutes. While the leeks are cooking, make the sauce.

Melt the butter in a saucepan, take the pan off the heat and add the flour and stir to make a roux. Heat the milk and pour on to the roux and stir until it is smooth, add salt and pepper, return to the heat, and, stirring all the time, bring to the boil, and cook the flour mixture for a minute or two. Check the seasoning.

When the leeks are cooked, drain well and arrange in a serving dish, spoon the sauce over the middle of them so that you can see the tops and bottoms of the leeks.

Braised Red Cabbage

1 red cabbage about 750 g/1½ lb
1 large onion
2 medium cooking apples
butter
salt and pepper
1 tablespoon sugar
3 tablespoons water
3 tablespoons vinegar

Trim the cabbage, cut into quarters, remove the core and slice fairly finely. Have ready a pan of boiling water, put in the shredded cabbage, and boil for 1 minute only, then drain. The cabbage will be blue at this stage, when the vinegar is added it will return to its red colour. Peel and slice finely the onion. Peel, core and slice the apples. Melt some butter in a pan and cook the onion and apple in it for a few minutes.

Rub the inside of a large ovenproof casserole with the butter, put in half the cabbage, the onion and apple and then the rest of the cabbage. Add the salt and pepper, the sugar and the water and vinegar. Cover with a piece of buttered paper, put on the lid and place in the oven, 170°C/325°F/Gas Mark 3, for 1½ to 2 hours.

* Red cabbage can be made the day before and reheated. It also freezes well.

Apple Upside-Down Sponge

For the topping:
75 g/3 oz/⅓ cup butter
100 g/4 oz/¾ cup soft brown sugar
750 g/1½ lb cooking apples

For the sponge:
75 g/3 oz/⅓ cup butter
75 g/3 oz/⅓ cup caster sugar
1 egg (size 3/large)
100 g/4 oz/1 cup self-raising flour
2 tablespoons milk

First prepare the topping. Melt the butter in a deep-sided sandwich tin 20 cm/8 in and add the sugar, mix until blended and coat the inside of the tin with the mixture. Leave on one side while the apples are prepared. Peel, core, quarter and slice the apples and arrange the slices in the greased tin.

Now make the sponge. Cream the butter, add the sugar and cream until they are light. Beat in the beaten egg and fold in the sifted flour with the milk. It should be a soft mixture. Spread this over the apples and put into a preheated oven, 180°C/350°F/Gas Mark 4 for about 1 hour.* Leave for a few minutes before turning out on to a plate. This pudding is good served either hot or cold, and is delicious served with cream.

As an alternative to the apple upside-down pudding serve a selection of cheeses with biscuits, and a bowl of fresh fruit.

* Freeze at this stage.

Christmas Buffet (illustration page 79)

As we have already talked about turkey, cranberry sauce, etc. for the Thanksgiving party, Diana thought ideas for a Christmas buffet would make a more interesting contribution to this book than another dinner menu.

For the food I have chosen two special favourites of the late Constance Spry, both appropriate for this occasion, devilled turkey legs and spiced beef. Both are simple to do, but as the beef has to be marinated it is important to get started in plenty of time as it needs a few days of preparation before you cook it.

Savoury pancakes are such a wonderful standby—they freeze well and have so many interesting fillings that they have a place here, even if you don't use them for this particular occasion. But, in fact, it is good to have a choice of hot or cold food if you are having a buffet, especially in winter.

Here the mince pies are attractively decorated and those with the cut-outs look so tempting that they are my special choice, particularly as they have a little less pastry! The custard is part of my family Christmas fare and it has been used for generations. I only use it for Christmas pudding or mince pies. It is, quite simply, a custard cooked with a bay leaf and topped with a sprinkle of cinnamon. It has a beautiful smooth taste and for me it means Christmas.

Presentation of food plays such an important part in entertaining that good and practical ideas are worth remembering and this half pineapple as a holder for fruit salad is a good example.

For the buffet centrepiece I used a two-tier vase. These are not matching vases and you can make it up for yourself with, perhaps, two comport vases (dishes with stems) which may be part of a dessert service, or build it up with two soup plates supported by two heavy wine glasses to provide the stems necessary for the elegant effect you want to achieve. There is some very good sticky plasticine-like adhesive called 'Oasis Fix' and I would recommend putting a little of this round the rim of each glass so that in no way could it slip and so upset the balance of the container. For one-off occasions like this which are not going to last long, there is no reason why you should not erect a 'Heath Robinson' type container that gives the effect without any great expense. But remember they must be firm and workable, even if only temporary.

Wet and dry Oasis, sold in different colours has made flower arranging much easier these days. I used dry Oasis here, cutting a piece from a large square so that it fitted tightly across the vase, to make perfectly sure that it would not slip about. There are heavy Oasis holders for the fix I have just mentioned but be sure and secure it well. I covered the dry Oasis with some small pieces of box and stuck in some tangerines as they were about the right weight and I needed to get the balance right. Most of the fruit you can impale into the Oasis with cocktail sticks, looping the grapes round the stick and putting one end into the Oasis and the other in a tangerine. This holds them quite firm. Many of the other little pieces went in on their own wires or stalks like the holly and the little Christmas baubles which already had wires on them when they were bought. This may seem rather a strange combination of fresh and glittery bits but they completely made the arrangement. I tried it first with fruit only, but though pretty it missed out, somehow. The effect of these shiny bubbles gave all the highlights needed. This arrangement is a good example of the value of textures—the dull-skinned fruit, the living fresh leaves and the glittery balls all combine to make a lively and effective grouping. A large candle at the top gives added height and the light helps the whole arrangement. This could have been made on the lines of the cone we showed for the Hallowe'en party using either a polystyrene cone or one cut out of small mesh wire and then filled with crushed up pieces of Oasis.

Here is an idea for a pretty hanging decoration. Take two large pine cones, place them in a warm oven or linen cupboard to encourage them to open and then coat with a layer of clear varnish. This gives a nice glossy effect and helps keep the cones permanently open. Hammer a large-headed nail into the end of each cone and tie on the ribbons and these will take the weight of the hanging cones. The ribbons should be of varying lengths, one about 1 m/3 ft long and another about 60 cm/2 ft. Round the nail and the ribbon press a large walnut-sized piece of plasticine or florist's clay. Into this put short pieces of berried and variegated holly. If berries are scarce then put in some small red ribbon bows fixed on wire so that they will stick into the plasticine more easily. Any hanging decoration immediately becomes a focal point and gives an instant party feeling to the room. These cones are also ideal for hanging on the front door.

Spiced Beef (this must be started a week before cooking)

25 g/1 oz allspice berries
1 large bay leaf
25 g/1 oz saltpetre (this is not essential but it gives the meat a nice pinky colour)
75 g/3 oz/$\frac{1}{4}$ cup cooking salt
75 g/3 oz/$\frac{1}{2}$ cup soft brown sugar
2 cloves garlic
2.5 kg/5 lb beef, topside or silverside

For cooking the meat:
2 onions
2 carrots
1 stick of celery
bouquet garni

Pound the allspice berries and the bay leaf and mix in the salts and sugar. Peel the cloves of garlic, and cut into slices. Make slits in the beef with a sharp knife and insert the slices of garlic. Rub the spice mixture all over the meat, put in a deep covered dish and leave in a cool place for a week, rubbing in the spices daily and turning it round. The day before it is to be eaten, take it out and wrap it in a piece of muslin and tie up like a parcel.

Peel the onions and carrots and cut into quarters, cut the celery into chunks. Put the meat into a large pan with the vegetables and the bouquet garni, cover with cold water and bring to the boil, simmer gently for 3 to 4 hours until the meat is tender. Allow it to cool slightly then take it out of the liquid, put it in a deepish dish, cover with a plate and press it down with a 2 kg/4 lb weight on top. Leave overnight.

To serve, put on to a board, and cut into not too thin slices.

Devilled Turkey Legs

For the marinade:
150 ml/$\frac{1}{4}$ pint/generous $\frac{1}{2}$ cup oil
2 tablespoons Worcestershire sauce
2 tablespoons tomato ketchup
1 dessertspoon made mustard
1 teaspoon sugar
1 teaspoon anchovy essence
salt and pepper

2 turkey legs

Mix all the ingredients for the marinade together. Put the turkey legs into a dish and pour over the marinade and leave overnight. Transfer the legs and marinade to a roasting tin and bake in the oven 190°C/375°F/Gas Mark 5 for about an hour or until the legs are cooked, basting them occasionally. The length of time they will take to cook will depend on the size and thickness of the legs. To serve the legs, arrange in a dish, pour over the marinade and cut the meat off in slices.

Coleslaw (to serve with the beef and the turkey legs)

1 white cabbage
2 large carrots
1 eating apple (red skinned if possible)
25 g/1 oz/$\frac{1}{4}$ cup roughly chopped walnuts

boiled dressing (see next recipe)

Cut the cabbage into four, take out the centre core, and shred the leaves finely. Peel the carrots and grate them into the cabbage. Quarter apples, remove the core, slice and add to the cabbage. Add the walnuts and mix well together. Pour over enough of the dressing to coat everything and mix well. This salad improves if allowed to stand for a little while to mature before being served.

Boiled Dressing

1 tablespoon sugar
1 dessertspoon flour
1 teaspoon salt
1 teaspoon mustard powder
1 tablespoon water
150 ml/$\frac{1}{4}$ pint/generous $\frac{1}{2}$ cup water
150 ml/$\frac{1}{4}$ pint/generous $\frac{1}{2}$ cup vinegar
1 egg
15 g/$\frac{1}{2}$ oz/1 tablespoon butter
cream or evaporated milk

Mix all the dry ingredients together and mix to a paste with a tablespoon of water. Put into a saucepan with the rest of the water and the vinegar, bring to the boil, stirring all the time and cook for about 5 minutes. Beat the egg thoroughly, pour on the hot mixture, add the butter and beat thoroughly. Cover and leave to get cold. When cold dilute with the cream or evaporated milk. This sauce keeps well in a screwtop jar in the refrigerator.

Savoury Pancakes

The pancake batter:
100 g/4 oz/1 cup plain flour
1 egg
1 egg yolk
300 ml/$\frac{1}{2}$ pint/1$\frac{1}{4}$ cups milk
1 tablespoon oil

Sift the flour into a basin and make a well in the centre and put into it the egg and the egg yolk. Slowly pour in the milk, stirring all the time and gradually incorporating the flour from round the edge. When half of the milk has been added, stir in the oil and beat until smooth. Add the remaining milk and leave to stand for about 30 minutes before making the pancakes. The batter should have the consistency of single cream so if it is thicker, add a little more milk.

To cook the pancakes. Have ready a small frying pan, about 18 cm/7 in in diameter (if possible, used only for making pancakes or for omelettes). Put a little oil into the pan and heat. When it is really hot, hold the frying pan in your left hand, pour in a small ladleful of the batter and at the same time turn the pan round so that the batter coats the base of the pan. The first pancake is really a test pancake, to check if the batter is of the correct consistency, and helps you judge how much batter is needed to make a thin pancake. Cook the pancake until it is a good brown colour underneath, then using a palette knife, slip it under the pancake and turn it over to cook for a few seconds. Turn the pancake out on to a wire rack. Make the other pancakes in the same manner, stacking them on top of one another.*

* The pancakes may be prepared in advance of the party; stack them in a pile with a piece of paper or polythene between each of them and freeze. Allow them to thaw for a few hours before stuffing them.

To stuff the pancakes. Spoon a little of the prepared stuffing into the centre of a pancake, fold in the edges to form a triangle and arrange in a serving dish. Cover with a piece of foil and reheat in the oven.

Any filling can be used to stuff the pancakes. The fillings given for the bouchées for the wedding reception and the cocktail party can be used, and below is another suggestion.

Smoked Haddock Filling

1 small onion
1 stick of celery
50 g/2 oz/$\frac{1}{4}$ cup butter
40 g/1$\frac{1}{2}$ oz/3 tablespoons plain flour
300 ml/$\frac{1}{2}$ pint/1$\frac{1}{4}$ cups milk
225 g/8 oz cooked smoked haddock fillet
salt and pepper

Peel the onion and finely chop it. Chop the celery also. Melt the butter in a pan, add the onion and celery and cook slowly until they are cooked without browning. Add the flour and stir well, pour on the milk, bring to the boil, stirring all the time, and cook for a few minutes. Skin the haddock and flake it, removing any bones that happen to be left in, then add it to the sauce. Check the seasoning then stuff the pancakes as described.

Mincemeat

450 g/1 lb/3 cups stoned raisins
450 g/1 lb/3 cups sultanas
450 g/1 lb/3 cups currants
450 g/1 lb/4 cups beef suet
50 g/2 oz/½ cup shredded almonds
350 g/12 oz cooking apples
½ teaspoon ground cinnamon
½ teaspoon ground nutmeg
350 g/12 oz/1½ cups demerara sugar
225 g/8 oz/1¼ cups mixed peel, chopped
grated rind and juice of 1 lemon
150 ml/¼ pint/generous ½ cup rum or brandy

First of all clean the fruit. Wash it in warm water, drain well and spread out on trays lined with two to three layers of absorbent kitchen paper, and leave to dry in a warm place (an airing cupboard is ideal). This must be done a day or two before it is needed. If butcher's suet is being used, either chop or grate it. Chop the raisins and sultanas and mix with the suet and currants, add the shredded almonds. Peel, core and chop the apples finely and add to the other ingredients with the spices, sugar, peel, lemon rind and juice, and the brandy or rum and mix all well together. Pack into clean jars and cover them with squares of polythene secured with a piece of string or screwtop lids. Store in a cool place for about a month before using. The quantities given will make about 3 kg/6 lb of mincemeat.

Mince Pies

225 g/8 oz/2 cups plain flour
150 g/5 oz/⅔ cup butter
25 g/1 oz/2 tablespoons lard or shortening
1–2 tablespoons cold water
1 egg yolk
750 g/1½ lb mincemeat (see recipe above)

Sift the flour into a bowl with a pinch of salt and rub in the butter and the shortening until it resembles breadcrumbs. As this is a rich pastry this will not take long and it is easy to overdo the rubbing in. Mix the water and the egg yolk together and add to the rubbed-in mixture and knead to make a dough. Leave in a cool place to chill for half an hour.

Take just over half of the pastry and roll it out, cut into rounds using a plain cutter and line the tartlet tins. Into the lined tins put a generous teaspoonful of mincemeat. Take the other half of the pastry and roll out and cut into rounds using a slightly smaller cutter than the one used for the bottoms. Cover some of the tarts with the whole plain rounds. If you have a star-shaped cutter or any other shape cut the centre out of the remaining rounds and cover some of the other tarts with these centreless rounds. Use the star-shaped centres to cover the remaining tarts. Brush the tops with water, sprinkle them with caster sugar and bake in the oven 200°C/400°F/Gas Mark 6 for 10–15 minutes. Leave for a few seconds in the tins before taking out and cooling on a wire rack. The quantities given will make about 30 mince pies.

Serve with the mince pies either brandy butter or bay flavoured custard.

* Mince pies can be made beforehand and either kept in an airtight tin for a week or frozen.

Brandy Butter

100 g/4 oz/$\frac{1}{2}$ cup *un*salted butter
100 g/4 oz/$\frac{1}{2}$ cup caster sugar
2–3 tablespoons brandy

Cream the butter to soften it then add the caster sugar and cream together until they are very light and fluffy. Gradually beat in the brandy, a little at a time until the desired flavour is obtained. Pile the brandy butter into a serving dish and chill.

* Brandy butter freezes well and can be kept for up to two months.

Bay Flavoured Custard

600 ml/1 pint/$2\frac{1}{2}$ cups milk
2 bay leaves
4 egg yolks
1 oz/2 tablespoons caster sugar
1 teaspoon custard powder or cornflour

Put the milk into a saucepan with the bay leaves and slowly bring it to boiling point and allow to infuse for a few minutes. Cream the yolks and the sugar together until they are thick, add the custard powder or the cornflour and mix in well. The addition of the custard powder or cornflour is not essential, but it helps to prevent the custard curdling. Remove the bay leaves from the milk and pour the milk on to the creamed yolks, stir well, rinse out the pan and return the custard to it. Stir over a very gentle heat until the custard thickens without boiling, otherwise it will curdle and you will then have a scrambled custard! Pour into a bowl to cool, stirring occasionally if serving cold. To serve hot pour into a warm jug or bowl. Decorate with a bay leaf.

Fresh Fruit Salad in a Half Pineapple

For the syrup:
100 g/4 oz/$\frac{1}{2}$ cup granulated or lump sugar
65 ml/$2\frac{1}{2}$ fl oz/5 tablespoons water

$\frac{1}{2}$ large pineapple
225 g/$\frac{1}{2}$ lb black grapes
225 g/$\frac{1}{2}$ lb white grapes
3 large oranges (seedless if possible)
1 grapefruit
2 eating apples
1 banana

To make the syrup put the sugar and water into a pan and stir until all the sugar has dissolved, boil for a few minutes then allow to get cold.

Prepare the fruit. Using a grapefruit knife (this is a knife with a serrated edge which curves at the bottom) cut the flesh out of the pineapple without making a hole in the skin, divide into segments and put into a bowl. Take the pips out of the grapes using a clean hair pin by pushing the rounded end into the grape, and pulling out the pips. Remove the skin and the pith from the oranges and the grapefruit with the grapefruit knife, divide into segments and put with the other fruit. Pour on the cold syrup. Do not add the banana until the last moment as it will go black fairly quickly. Quarter the apple, remove the core and slice into the fruit salad. Before serving, spoon the fruit into the empty pineapple shell. Have the bowl of fruit salad in the background so the pineapple can easily be topped up.

Index